Music Theory for Singers

Level Two

Second Edition

Sarah Sandvig

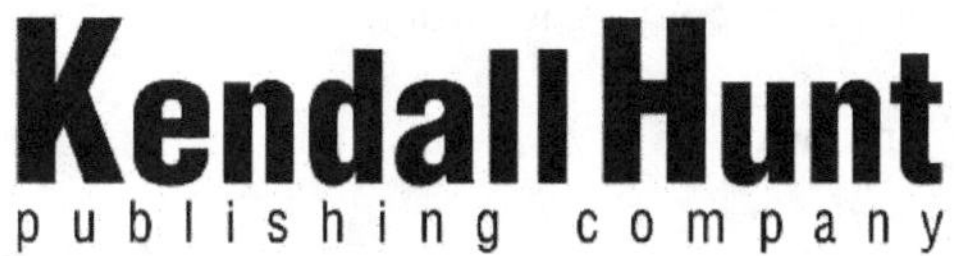

Cover image © Shutterstock, Inc. Used under license.
Back cover image and all keyboard images provided by the author.

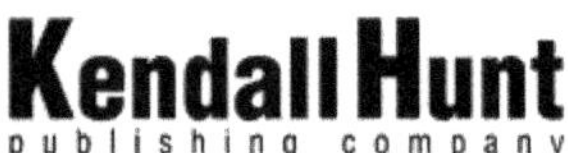

www.kendallhunt.com
Send all inquiries to:
4050 Westmark Drive
Dubuque, IA 52004-1840

ISBN 978-1-5249-1437-0

Published in the United States of America

FOREWORD

In Sarah Sandvig's *Music Theory for Singers*, voice students and their teachers finally have a singer-friendly primer for musicianship and music theory that is directly applicable to voice training. Mrs. Sandvig has capitalized on her experience as a successful private voice teacher to create this comprehensive workbook, which, in clear, concise language, lays out an easy-to-follow lesson plan progressing from basic through advanced skills. *Music Theory for Singers* is equally applicable in a college or high school classroom setting as in the private studio, and voice teachers will especially appreciate the inclusion of international musical terminology, and music history which their students are likely to encounter in vocal repertoire. For teens studying voice for the first time, as well as for life-long adult singers, *Music Theory for Singers* will become a valued adjunct to any level of vocal study.

Juliana Gondek
Metropolitan Opera soloist and
Prize-winning international recording artist
Professor and Chair, Division of Voice Studies
UCLA

I am beginning my first semester as a BFA Musical Theatre Major at The Boston Conservatory at Berklee. I used Sarah's theory books throughout high school from levels 5 through 10, and they have prepared me immensely for this first semester – and beyond. For example, I recently went through a music theory and sight singing placement test: I was so amazed how comfortable I felt with both the written and singing portions. It was everything I had already learned from these theory books – key signatures, scales, rhythm, solfege, and more. In addition, I became so familiar with the fundamentals of music and a piano keyboard (even through utilizing the vocal theory books) I was able to test out of a whole year of beginner piano. All of this creates the possibility for me to move on to higher levels and be more challenged than if I had to start from the basics. Not to mention all of the composers and terms that are necessary knowledge to be successful in professional music classes and settings. It feels good to know that if I am ever unsure about what I am learning in class, my theory books are right there on the bookshelf to help me out.

Sofia Ross
Musical Theatre Major
Boston Conservatory

Thank you to the following people for their help and guidance in writing these books: Mary Beard, Melissa Caldretti, Sally Curry, Sharlae Jenkins, Vanessa Parvin, Connie Venti & my dad, Ken Watson.

Thank you to my husband Darren and sons Aiden & Caleb for their love, support and patience throughout this writing process.

NOTE TO TEACHER:
These books are a supplement to private, group or classroom voice lessons, and though I feel they can stand alone, they are not meant as a replacement for a good teacher who ensures student learning and understanding of music theory, history, and sight-singing. Each book includes reviews of subjects with a review test (with answers) at the end. You may also purchase the Answer Key, which has answers to all pages in each level, 1-10. Composers, terms, IPA and solfege are unique elements of these books that make them especially helpful for singers.

I hope these books are a useful addition to the many tools you already utilize to teach young singers in your studio or classroom.

TABLE OF CONTENTS

MUSIC THEORY FOR SINGERS

LEVEL 2

Reveiw of Concepts in Level 1

The Staff: Review

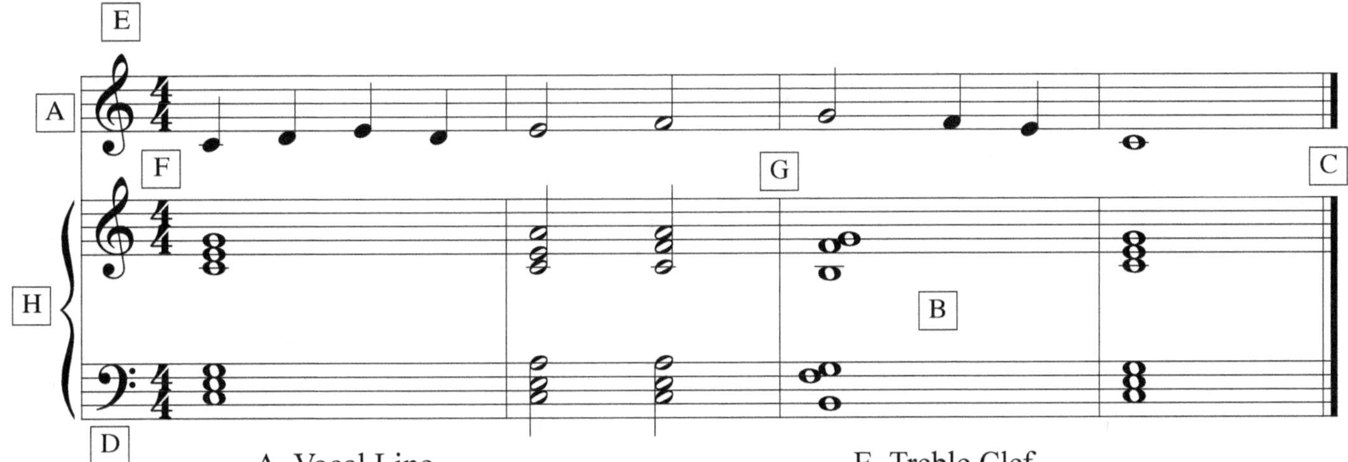

A. Vocal Line

B. Measure

C. Double Bar Line

D. Bass Clef

E. Treble Clef

F. Time Signature

G. Bar Line

H. Grand Staff

Rhythm: Review

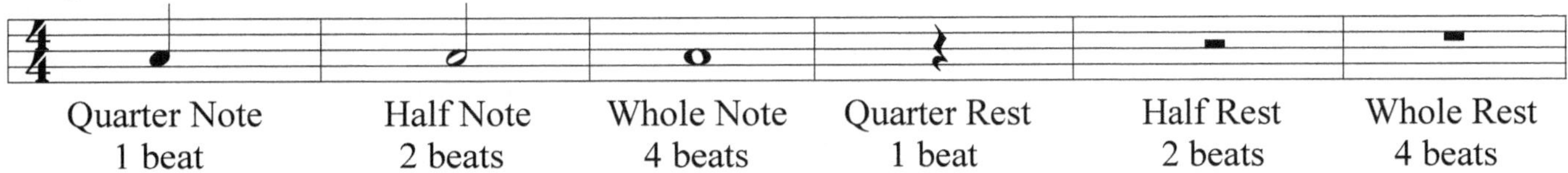

Time Signature: Review

Top number = 4 beats per measure. Bottom number = a quarter note gets 1 beat.

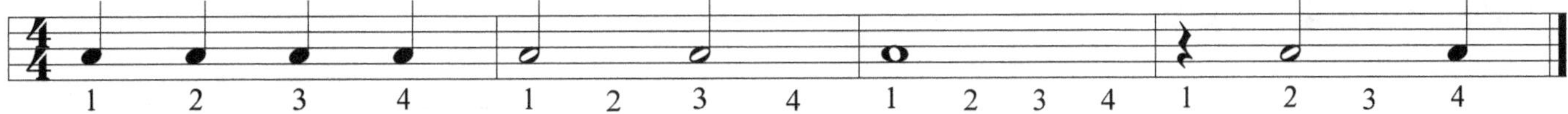

Top number = 3 beats per measure. Bottom number = a quarter note gets 1 beat.

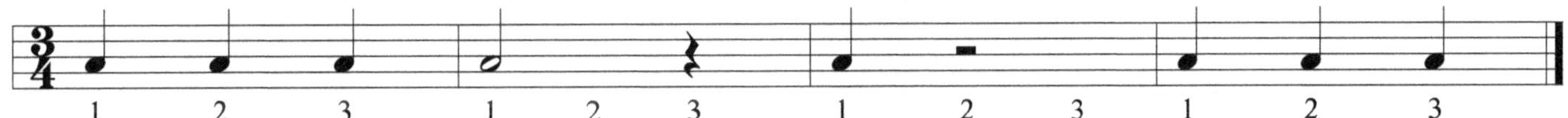

Top number = 2 beats per measure. Bottom number = a quarter note gets 1 beat.

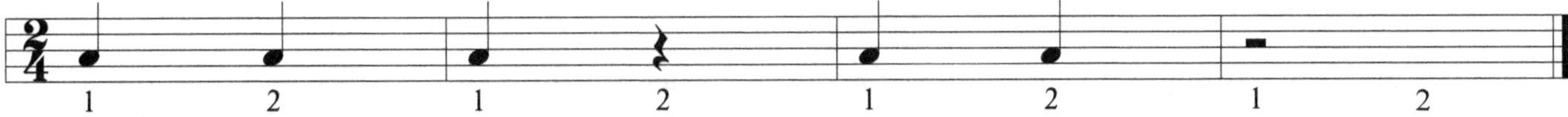

Note Review

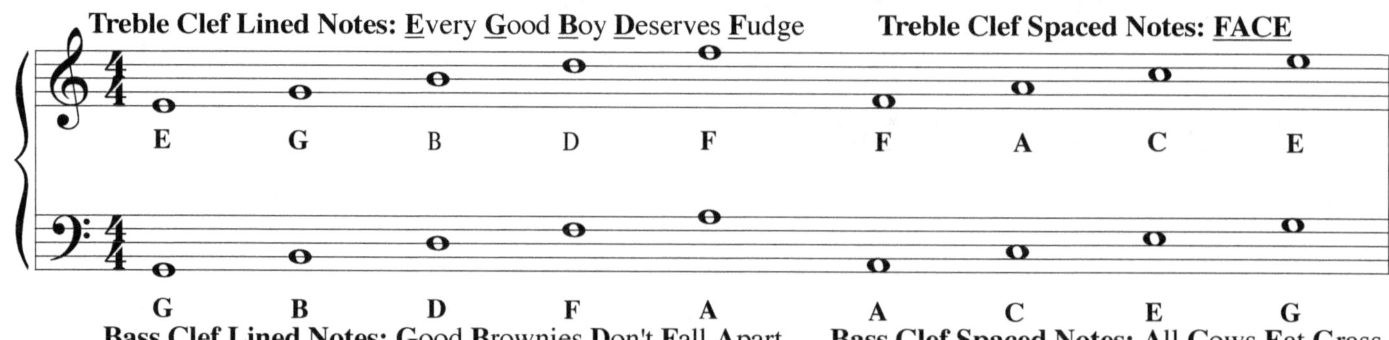

Key Signature & Triad Review

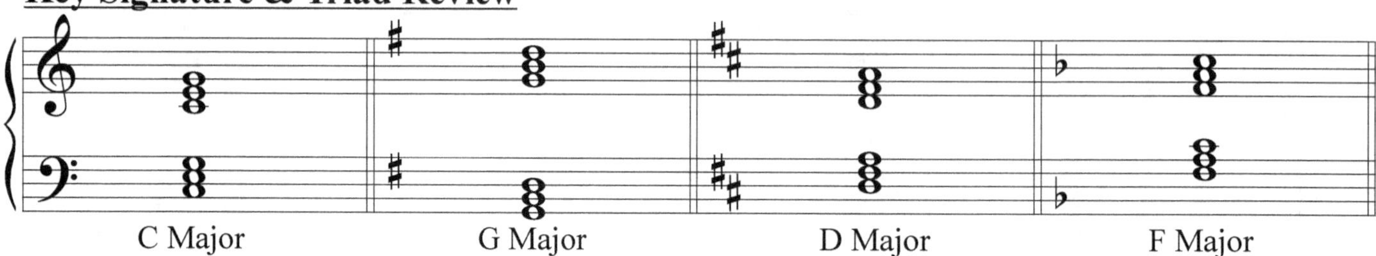

Interval Review

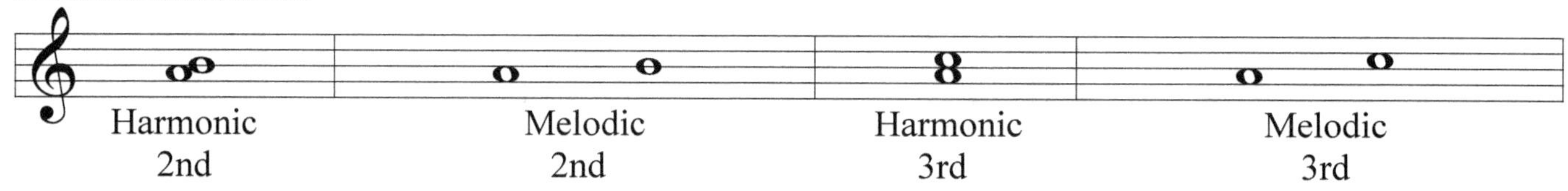

IPA/Diction Review

IPA SYMBOL	SOUND IN ENGLISH WORD	IPA SPELLING OF WORD	TONGUE/LIPS PLACEMENT
i	ski	[ski]	Center of tongue is high Lips relaxed
ɛ	led	[lɛd]	Low tongue Lips relaxed
ɑ	father	[ˈfɑðər]	Low tongue Lips relaxed
o	obey	[oʊˈbeɪ]	Low tongue, tip behind bottom teeth Rounded lips
u	goose	[gus]	Low tongue, tip behind bottom teeth Rounded lips

Sight-Singing Review

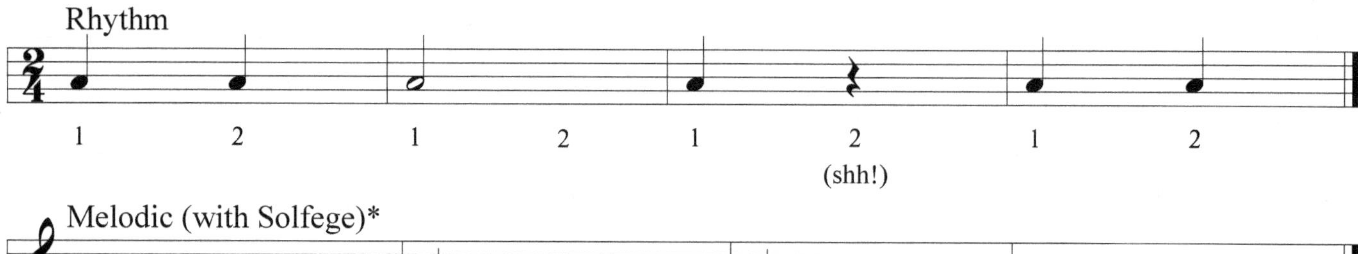

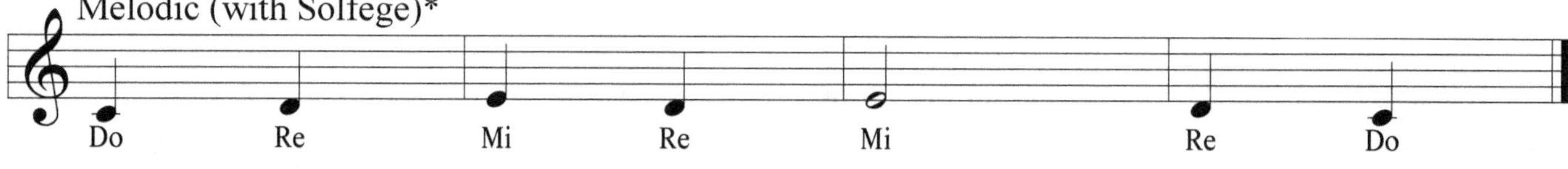

*The Solfege system assigns a syllable to each note of a scale starting with Do. The syllables used for a major scale are: Do Re Mi Fa Sol La Ti Do. Solfege has been in existence for more than 1,000 years!

Lesson 1: Musical Symbols on the Staff

The Tie

A Tie is a curved line connecting two notes of the **same** pitch, which combines their value. For example, a quarter note tied to another quarter note is sung and held for two counts… Look at the examples below:

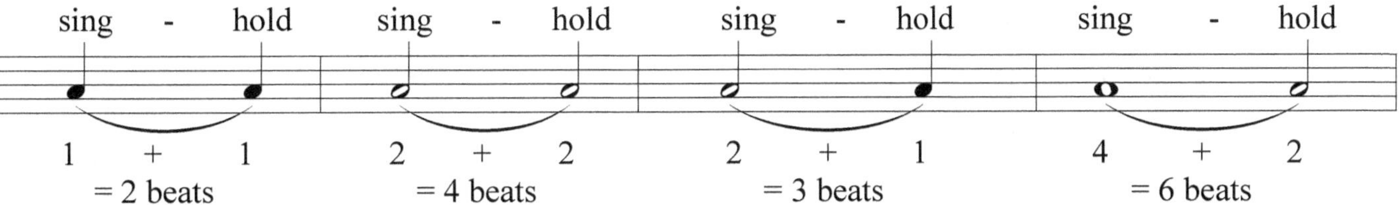

In the melodic example below, notice how the tied note A ("Mi") is sung in the first measure then held into the second measure.

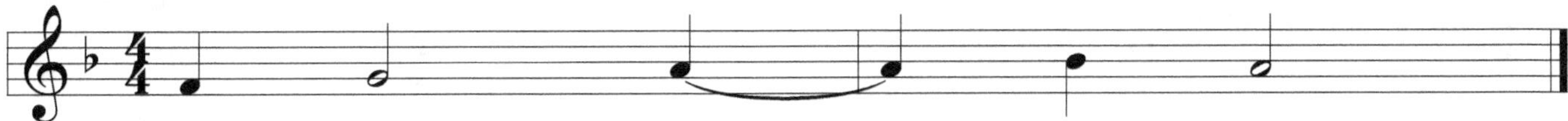

*The Slur

A Slur is a curved line connecting two or more **different** notes, indicating to sing smoothly, or legato. Slurs divide music into phrases. Look at the example of slurs below.

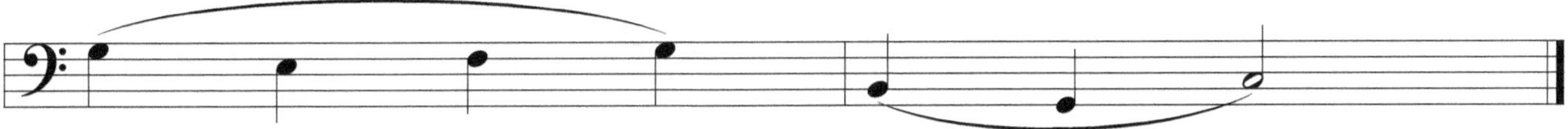

Staccato

The opposite of singing legato is staccato (a term covered in Level 1). Staccato notes are to be sung short and detached and indicated by a dot over or under the note head.

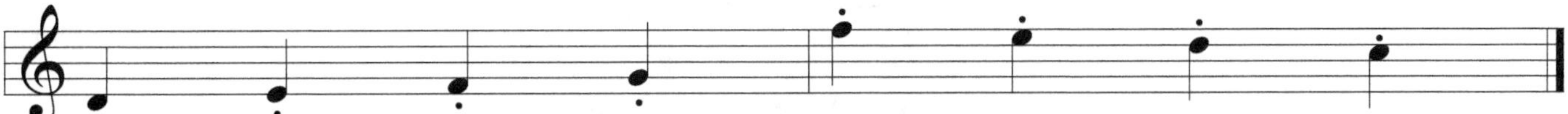

There is an example of staccato notes, a tie and a slur in the example below.

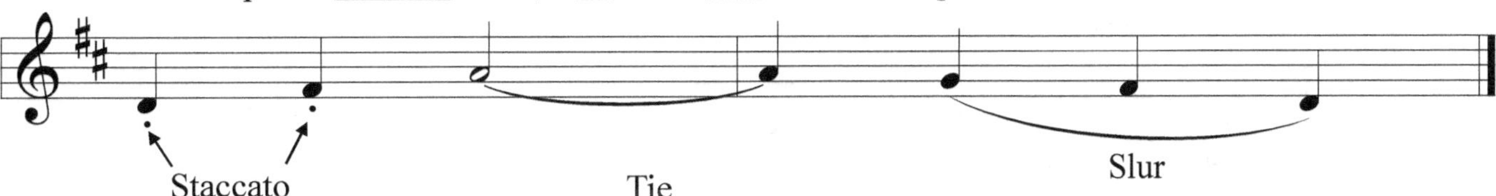

Remember a tie is between 2 of the same notes, while a slur creates musical phrases with different notes.

*While most of what we sing is legato, slurs are especially important in classical music, namely Baroque, Classical, and Romantic period music where the composers intentionally add in slurs for specific phrasing.

Review: Lesson 1

1. Circle "tie" or "slur" for each of the examples below.

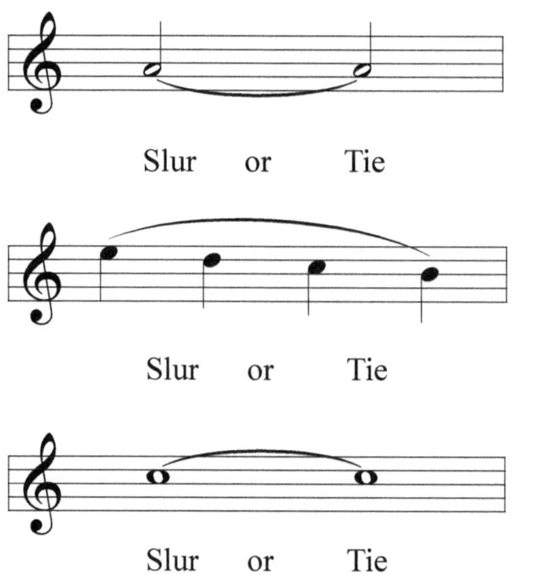

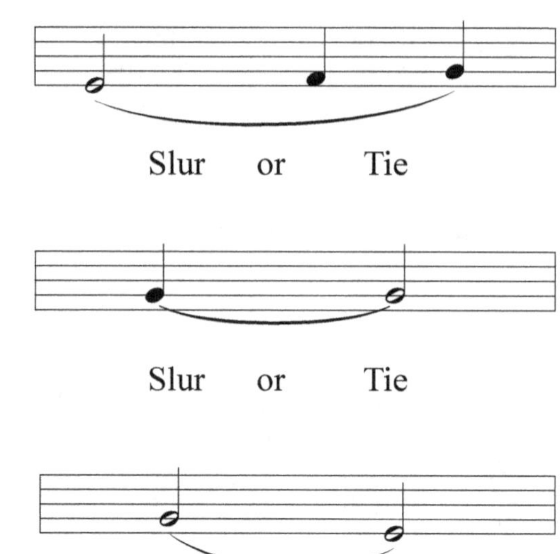

2. Check how many beats these tied notes receive in 4/4 time.

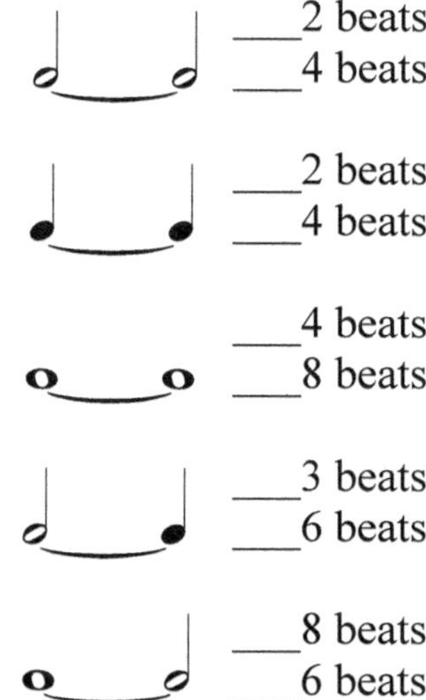

___2 beats
___4 beats

___2 beats
___4 beats

___4 beats
___8 beats

___3 beats
___6 beats

___8 beats
___6 beats

3. Add the tied notes together and write their total value below. In these examples, a quarter note gets one beat. The first one is done for you.

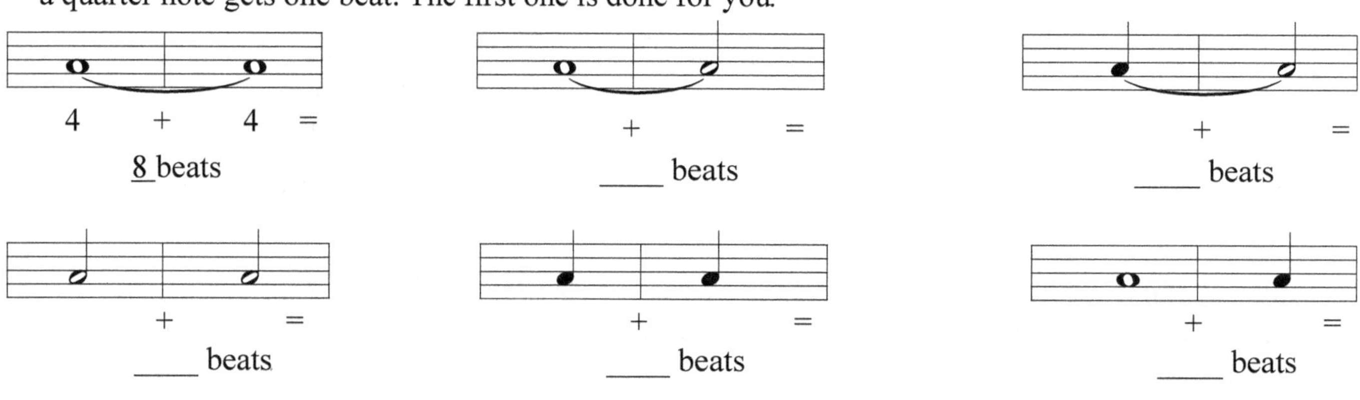

4. Add a **slur** over or under the notes in measures 1-2 and measures 3-4 in the examples below. Follow the directions (under/over) before each measure. Remember to connect the slurs to the note head, not the stem. The first one is done for you.

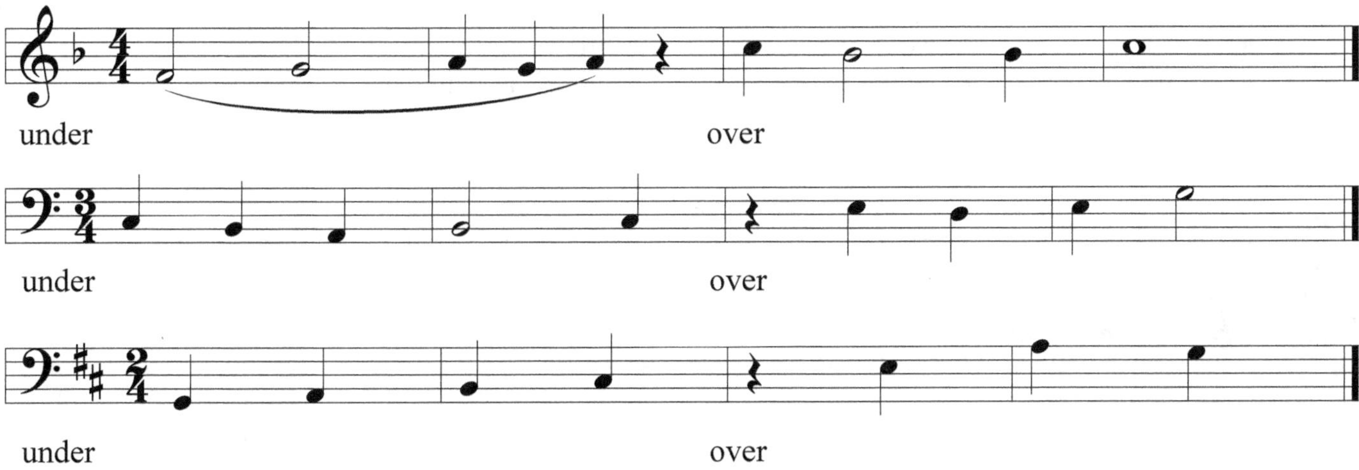

5. Add a **tie** between the 2 notes in the measures indicated. Remember to connect the tie to the note head, not the stem. The first one is done for you.

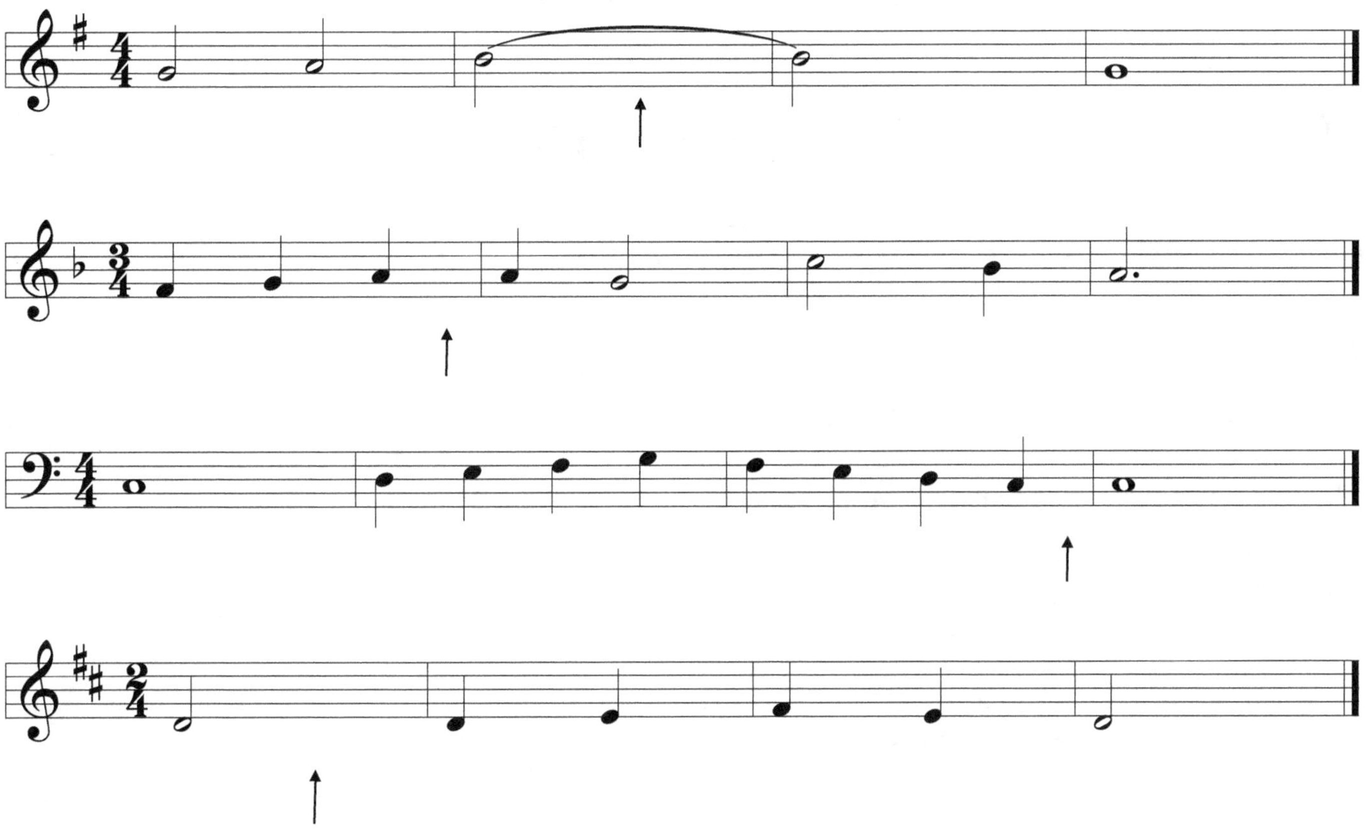

Lesson 2: The Repeat Sign/1st & 2nd Endings

The Repeat Sign

The Repeat Sign, indicated by two dots placed before or after a double bar line, indicates a repeat of the music. The singer would go back to the beginning and sing the example two times.

Example 1

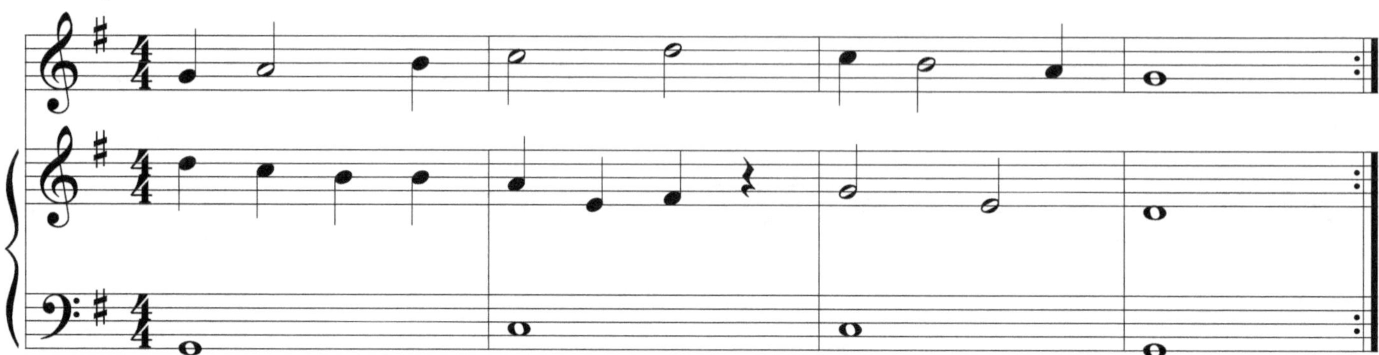

In the following example, the singer would sing measures 1-4, then measures 3-4 again. Only the measures within the repeat signs are repeated.
In other words, the order of measures in which they would be sung is: 1-2-3-4-3-4

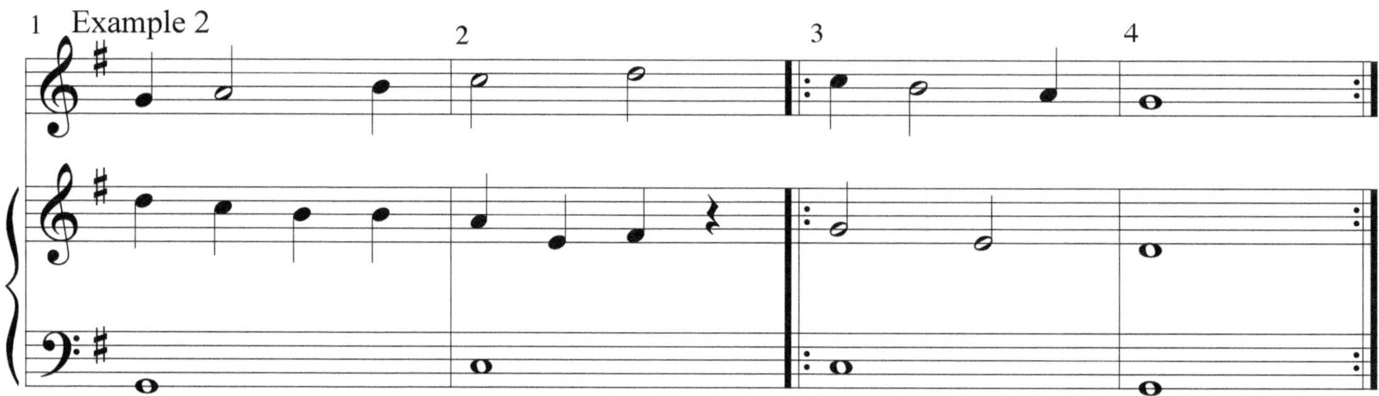

Example 3 shows how Example 2 would be sung.

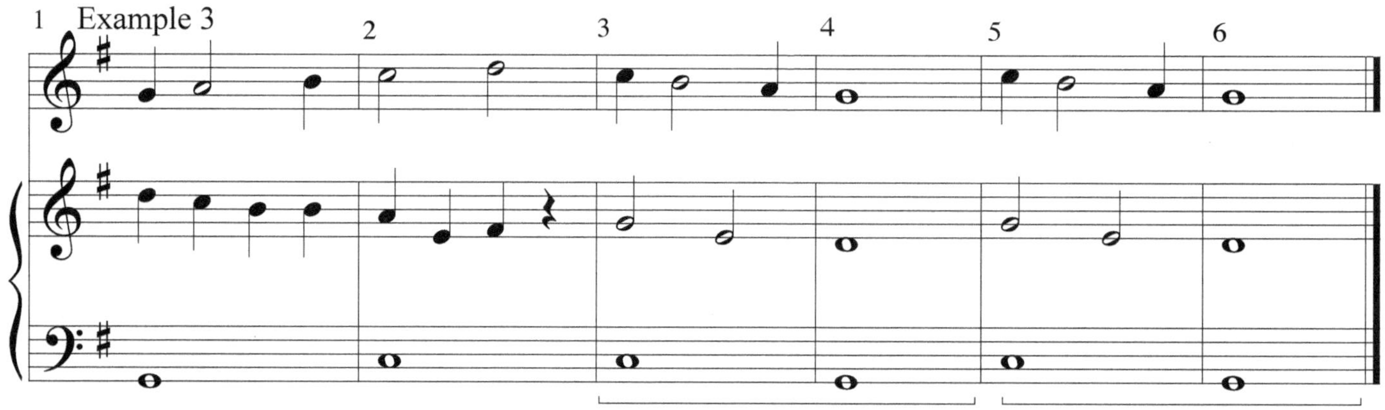

measures 3-4 from Example 2 repeat of measures 3-4

1st & 2nd Endings

Rather than writing repeating melodies out, composers often use 1st and 2nd endings to condense their scores (songs).

If you see 1st & 2nd endings while singing a song, you will sing the 1st ending first, then repeat to the beginning. When you get to these endings again, you skip the 1st ending and sing the 2nd.

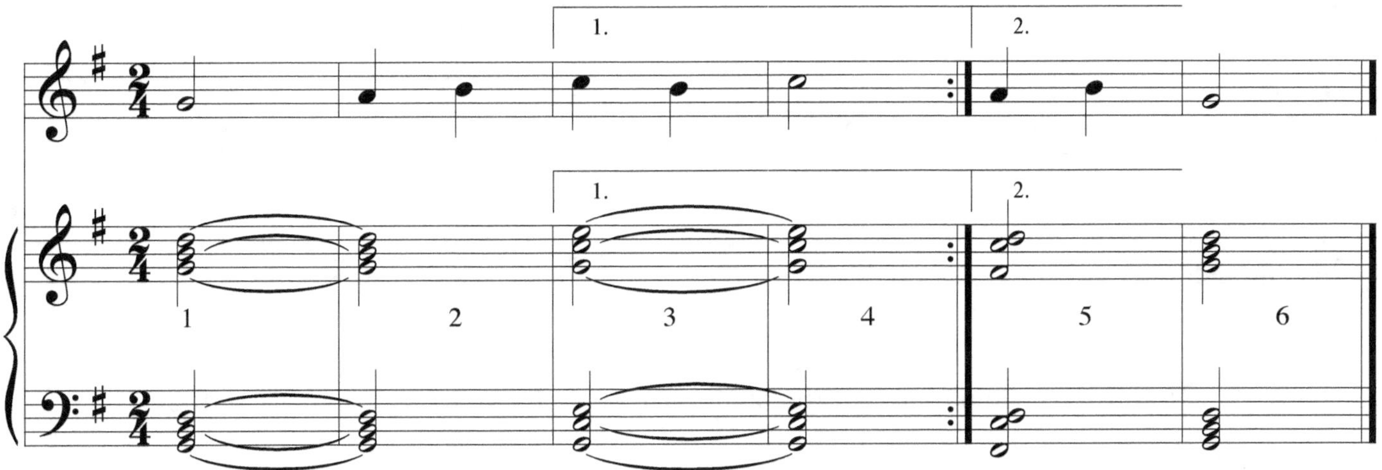

In the example above, the singer sings measures 1-4, then repeats back to the beginning. Next, the singer sings measure 1-2, skips measures 3-4, then sings measures 5-6.

The example below demonstrates how you would sing the example above.

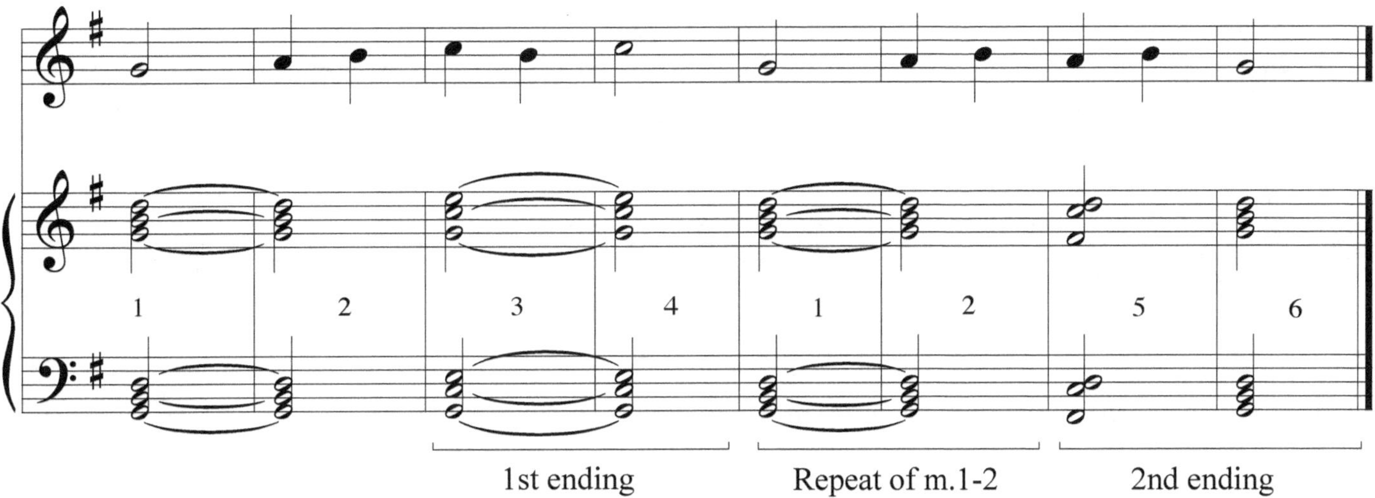

Review: Lesson 2

1. Add a repeat sign in all 3 staves in the last measure of the example below. Remember the top dot is above the middle line of the staff and the bottom dot is below the middle line of the staff.

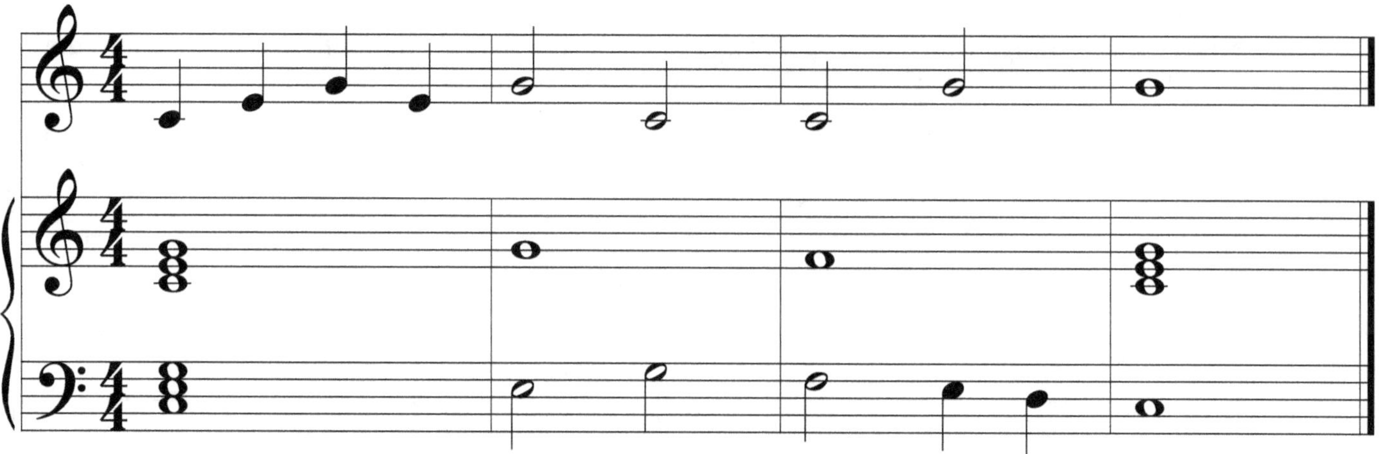

2. Look at the following examples, then write out how it would be sung on each blank staff below.

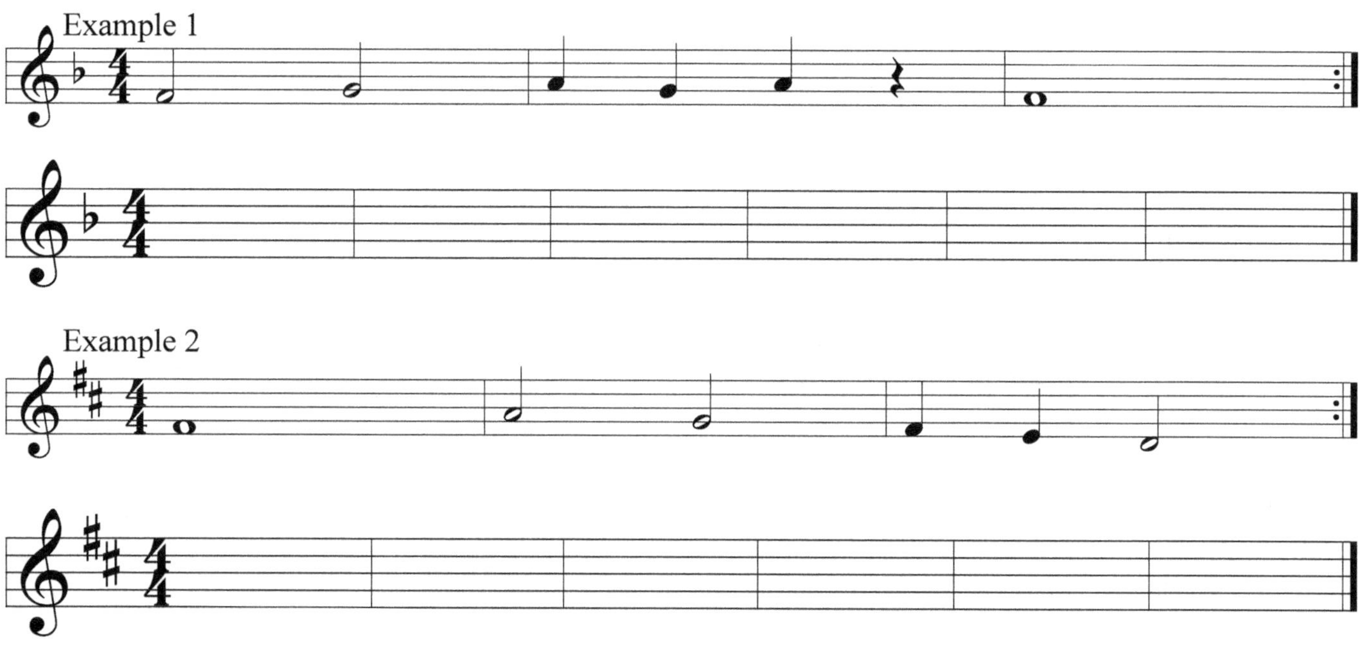

3. Write the measure numbers in the order in which they would be sung.

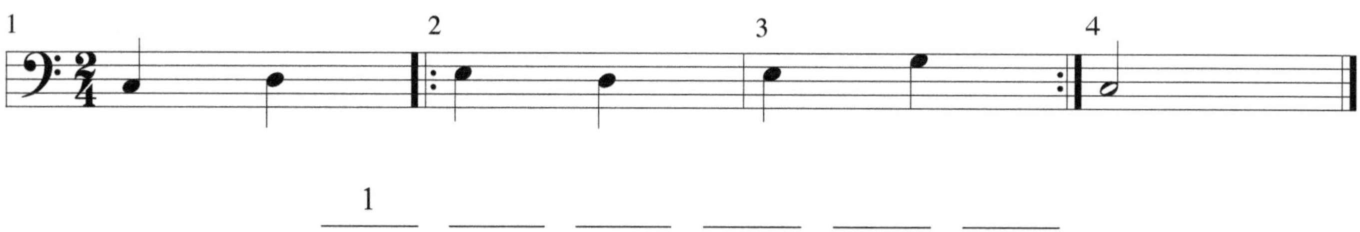

1 ______ ______ ______ ______ ______ ______

4. Write the measure numbers in the order in which they would be sung.

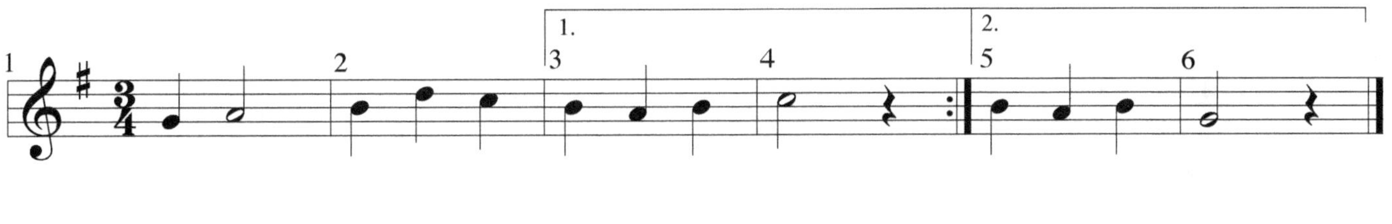

______ ______ ______ ______ ______ ______ ______ ______

5. Answer the questions about this musical example. Check your answers.

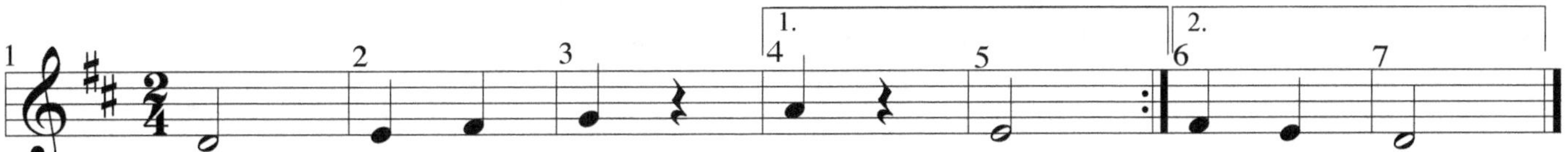

a. What two measures contain the 2nd ending?
___4 & 5
___6 & 7

b. What measure do you sing after measure 5?
___1
___6

c. Which measure do you sing before measure 6?
___5
___3

d. What key is this example in?
___G Major
___D Major

6. Look at the following example, then write out how it would be sung on the blank staff below.

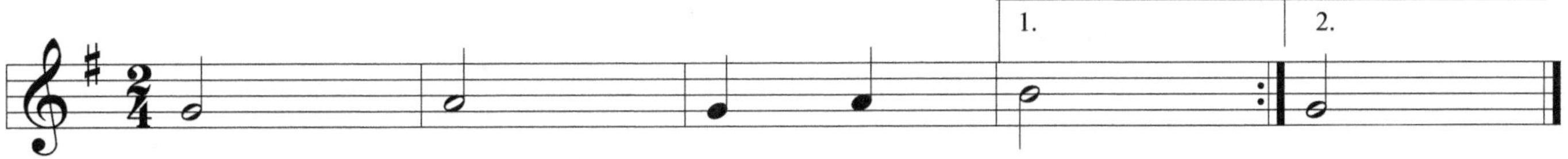

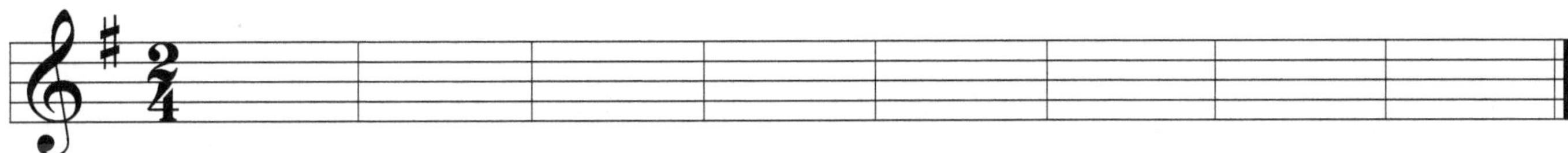

Lesson 3: Note & Rest Values

Dotted Half Note

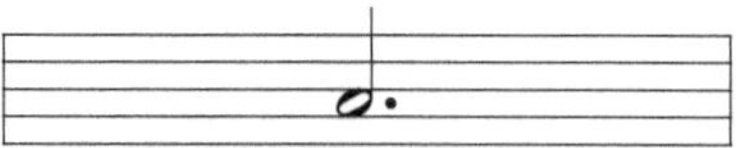

A dotted half note is sung for 3 beats.

Adding a dot to a note lengthens a note by half of its value.
For instance, a half note is worth 2 beats, so the dot is worth 1 beat.
Add the beats together, and a dotted half note is worth 3 beats.

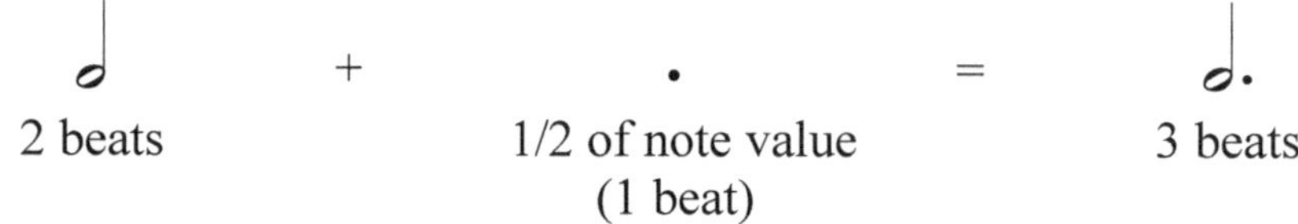

Dotted Half Rest

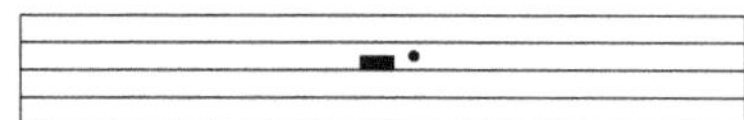

A dotted half rest is worth 3 beats of silence.

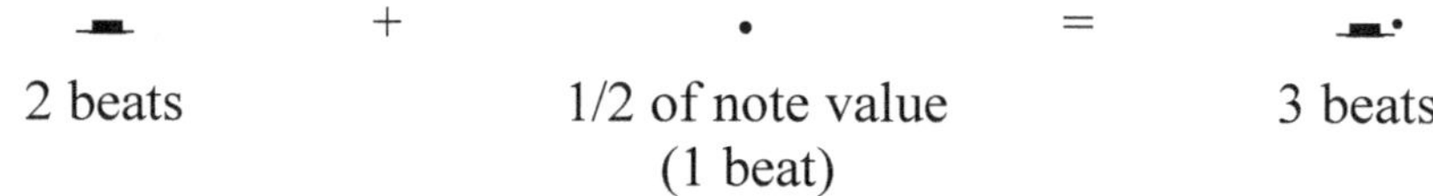

In a 3/4 time signature, a dotted half note fills an entire measure. However, a whole rest fills an entire measure regardless of the time signature. A whole rest thus means "rest for the whole measure."

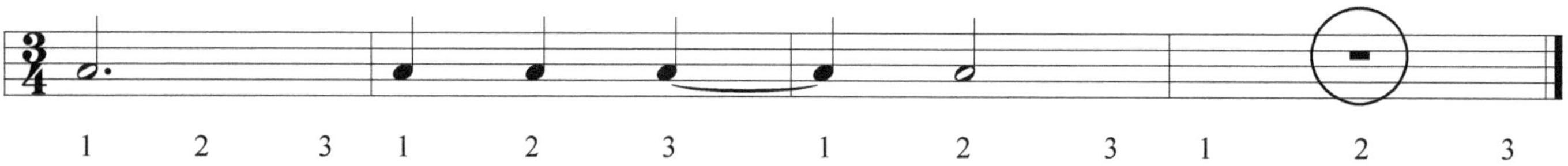

In some compositions, you may see a dotted half rest in place of a whole rest as well.

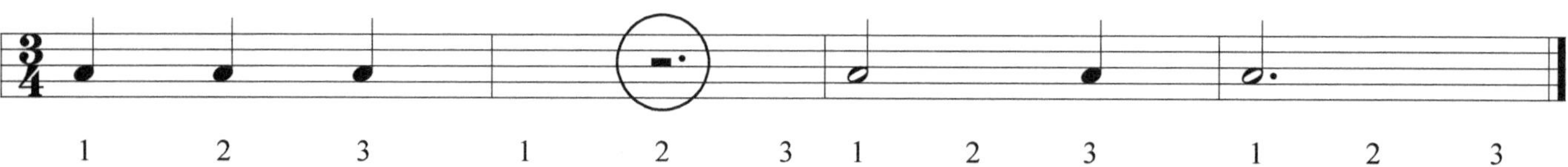

Review: Lesson 3

1. Check the correct counting for each of these examples.

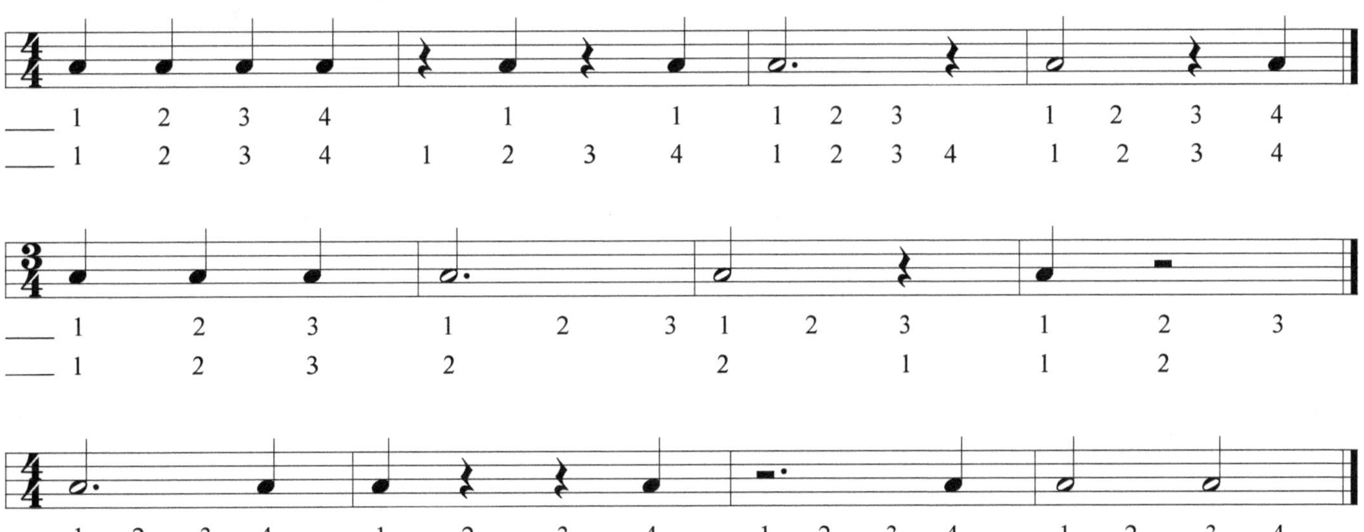

2. Check the correct number of beats each note or rest will receive in $\frac{4}{4}$ time.

3. Circle the correct name for each note or rest.

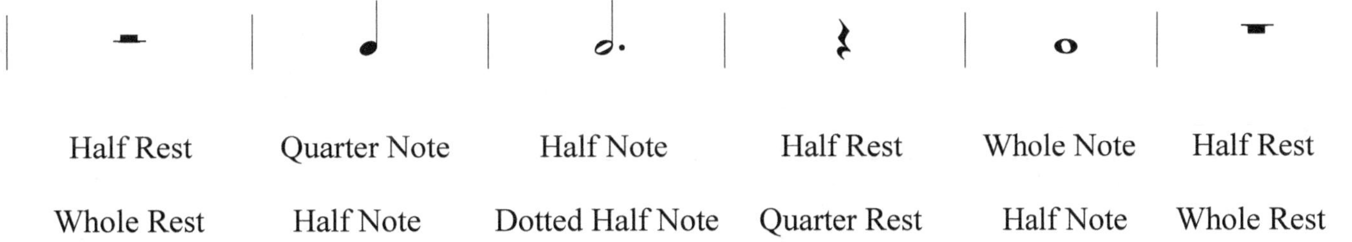

4. Write the beats under each note/rest in the following examples. Pay attention to the time signatures!

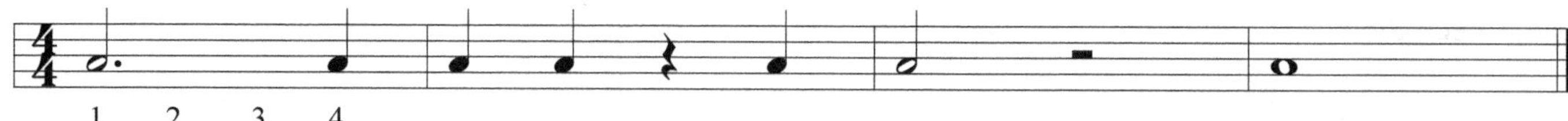

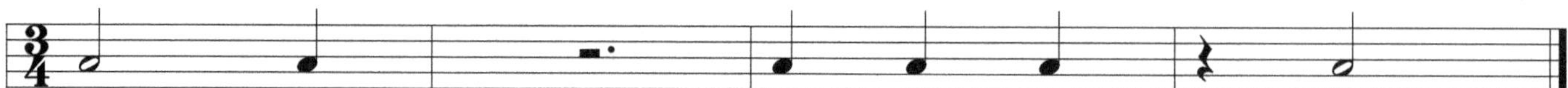

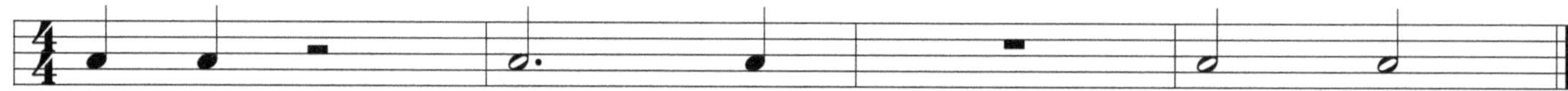

5. Add the 3 missing bar lines and a double bar line to the examples below.

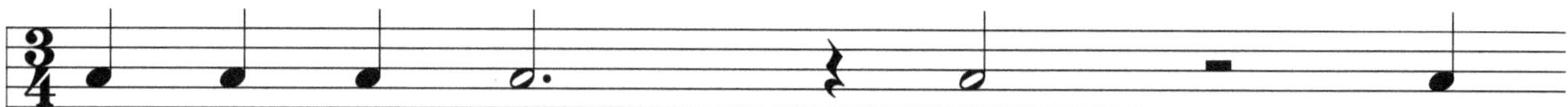

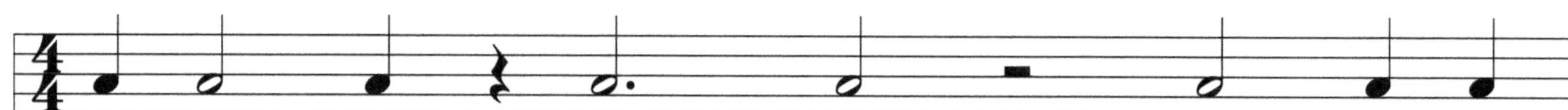

6. Add **one** missing note or rest to complete each measure in the examples below.

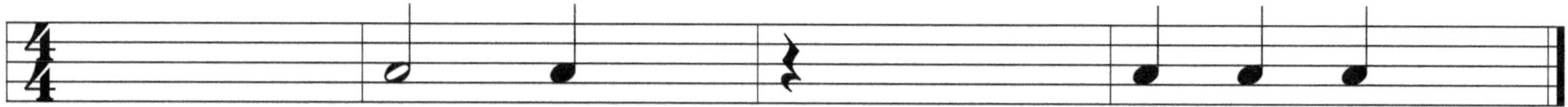

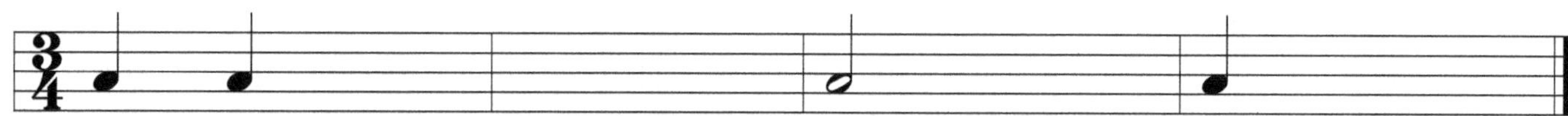

Lesson 4: Ledger Lines

Notes continue above and below the grand staff. Small segments of additional staff lines are called Ledger Lines.

If a note is sitting ABOVE or BELOW a ledger line, it is a space note.

If a note has a ledger line through the center of it, it is a line note.

In the following example, notes are written outside of the staff. Notice how when the notes get higher, the alphabet letters are in the correct order. When the notes get lower, the alphabet is backwards.

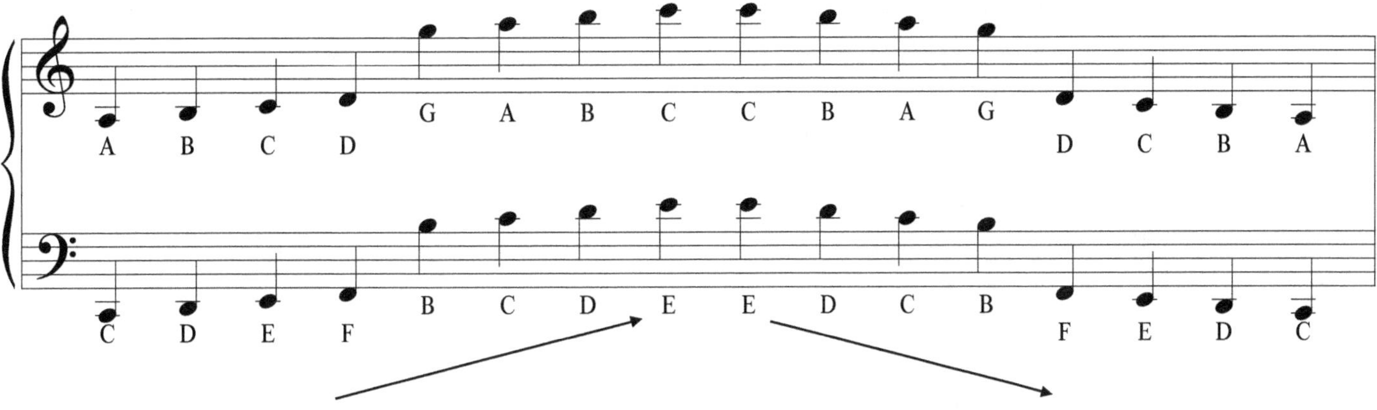

Here are the treble clef notes on the staff, including ledger line notes.

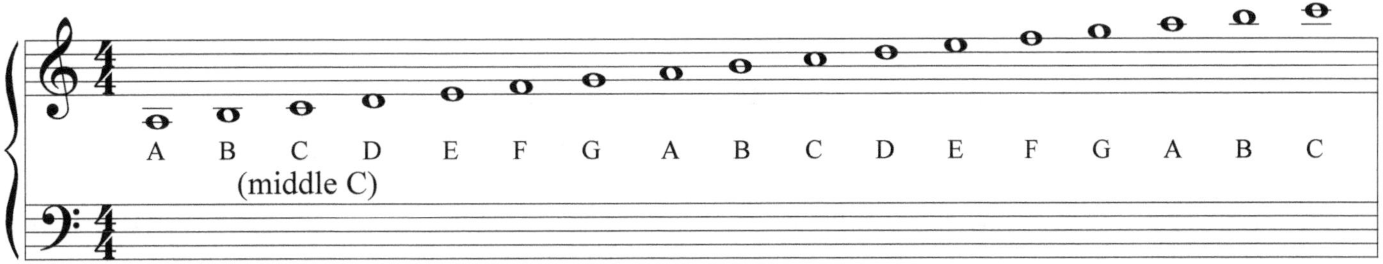

Here are the bass clef notes on the staff, including ledger line notes.

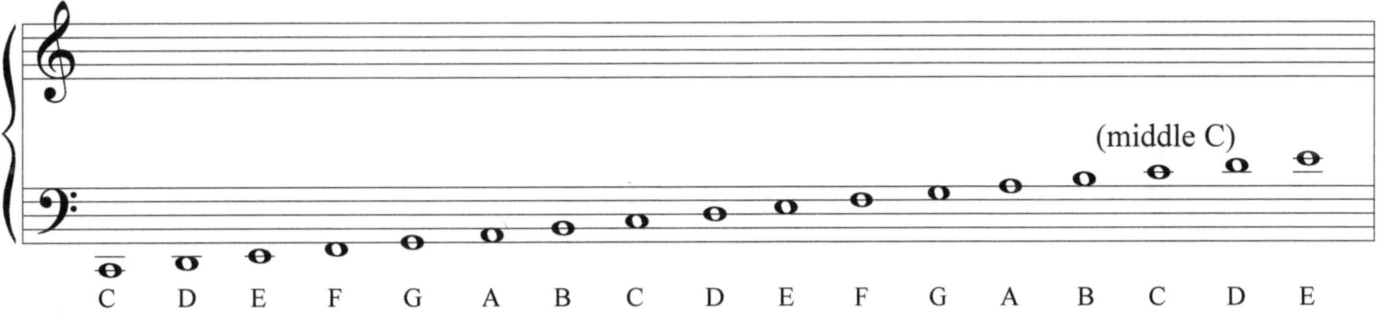

Review: Lesson 4

1. Name the following notes. Pay close attention to the clefs.

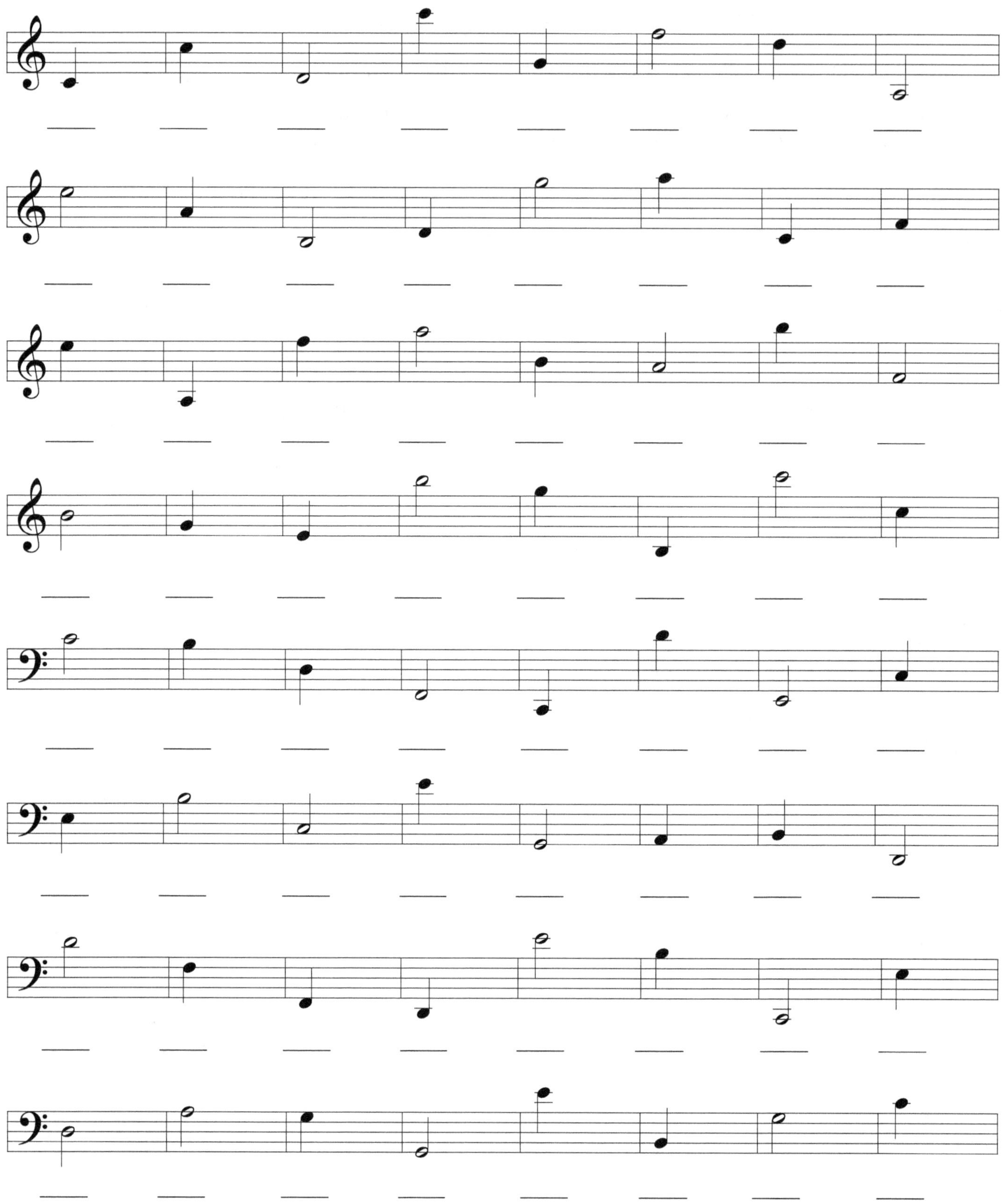

2. Draw the following notes. Use quarter notes and make sure your stems are going in the right direction.

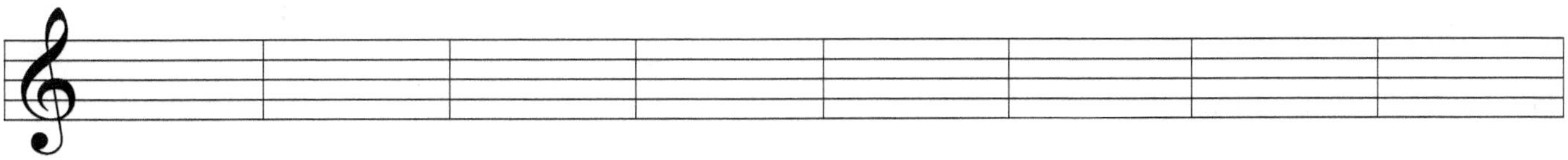

middle C	G	B	C	D	A	A	B
ledger line	above the staff	below the staff	above the staff	below the staff	above the staff	below the staff	above the staff

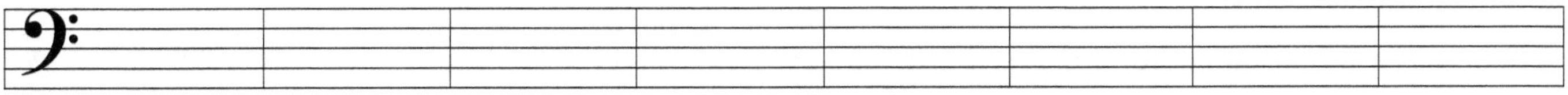

D	D	F	B	C	E	E	middle C
below the staff	above the staff	below the staff	above the staff	below the staff	above the staff	below the staff	ledger line

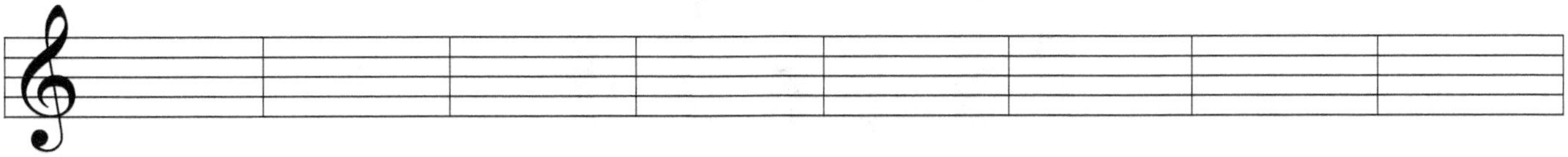

A	A	B	B	C	D	G	middle C
above the staff	below the staff	above the staff	below the staff	above the staff	below the staff	above the staff	ledger line

3. Write the letter name of each note.

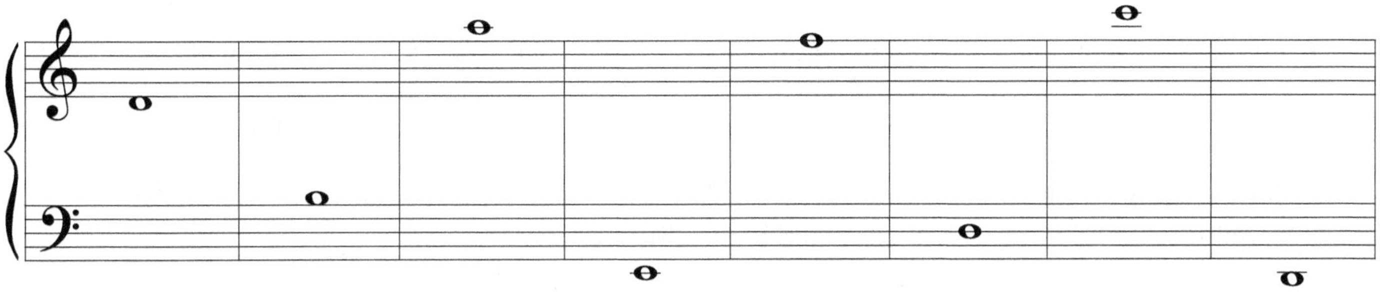

_____ _____ _____ _____ _____ _____ _____ _____

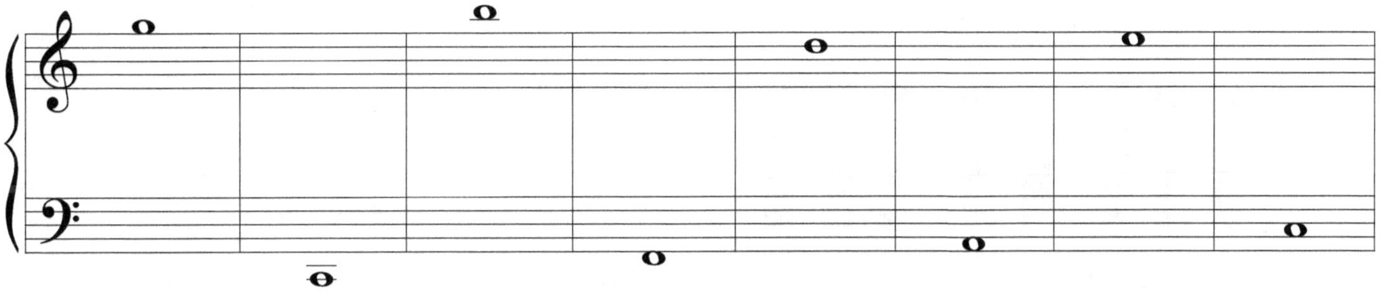

_____ _____ _____ _____ _____ _____ _____ _____

Lesson 5: Key Signatures

In music, a Key Signature is a series of sharp (♯) or flat (♭) symbols placed on the staff immediately after the Treble and Bass clefs. The Key Signature also creates the tonal center for a piece.

The key signature shows which notes are to be sung a half step higher (sharp) or a half step lower (flat) for the duration of the piece.

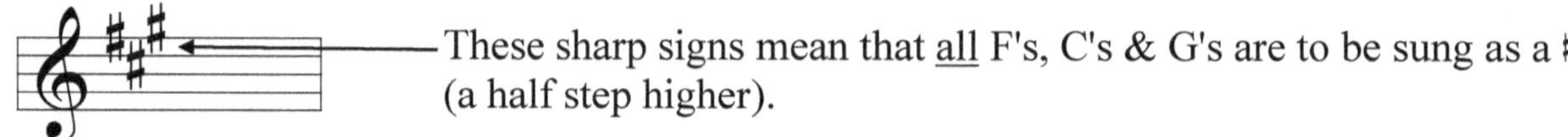

Key signature of A Major

A half step is the distance from one pitch the the very next pitch (up or down), while a whole step is comprised of 2 half steps (up or down). This is easy to see on a piano keyboard like the one below.

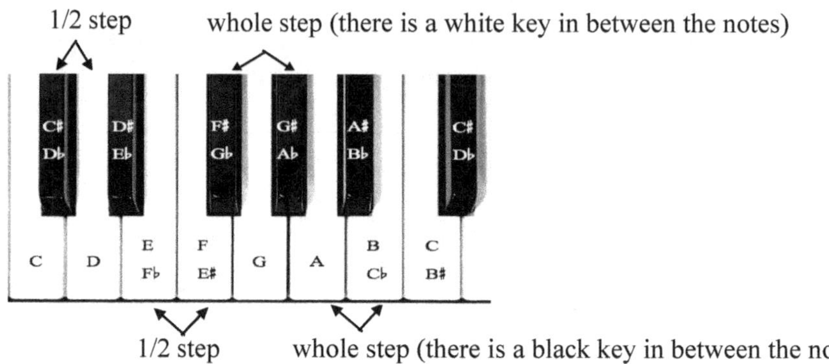

The key signature of A Major has an F♯, C♯ and G♯ because in order for it to sound Major (or happy), the notes must follow a specific pattern of half steps and whole steps.

The pattern of half steps and whole steps that make up a Major scale (8 notes) is as follows:

Whole - Whole - Half - Whole - Whole - Whole - Half (W - W - H - W - W - W - H)

Take a look at an A Major scale on the staff below. The C♯, F♯ & G♯ must be added in order for the formula (pattern of half steps and whole steps) to be correct.

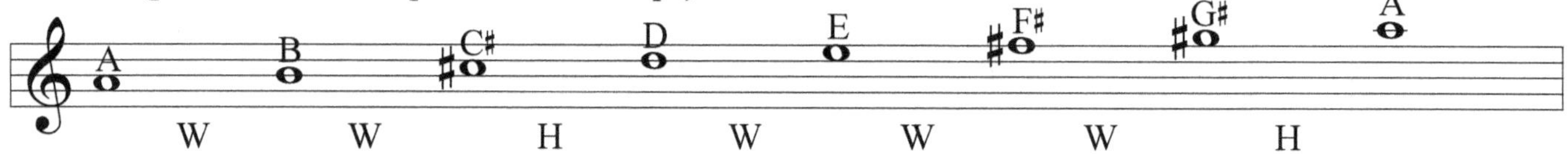

Here is what an A Major scale looks like on a piano keyboard.

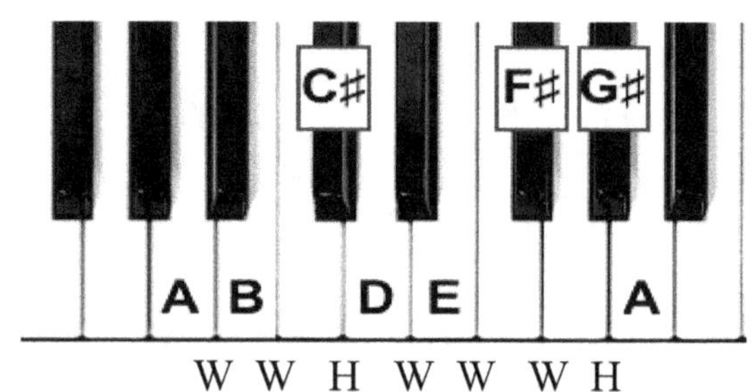

- A to B is a whole step (there is a black note in between, A to B consists of 2 half steps).
- B to C♯ is a whole step (we had to add the sharp because B to C would only be a half step, which wouldn't be correct in our Major scale formula).
- C♯ to D is a half step (no note in between, they are as close as they can be)
- D to E is a whole step
- E to F♯ is a whole step (there is a white key in between)
- F♯ to G♯ is a whole step (there is a white key in between)
- G♯ to A is a half step

In this Level, we are going to study 3 new key signatures: A Major, E Major & B Major. You learned C Major, G Major, F Major and D Major in Level 1.

Look at the Major scales below for these key signatures so you can see how the Major scale pattern, W-W-H-W-W-W-H adds the necessary accidentals (sharps/flats).

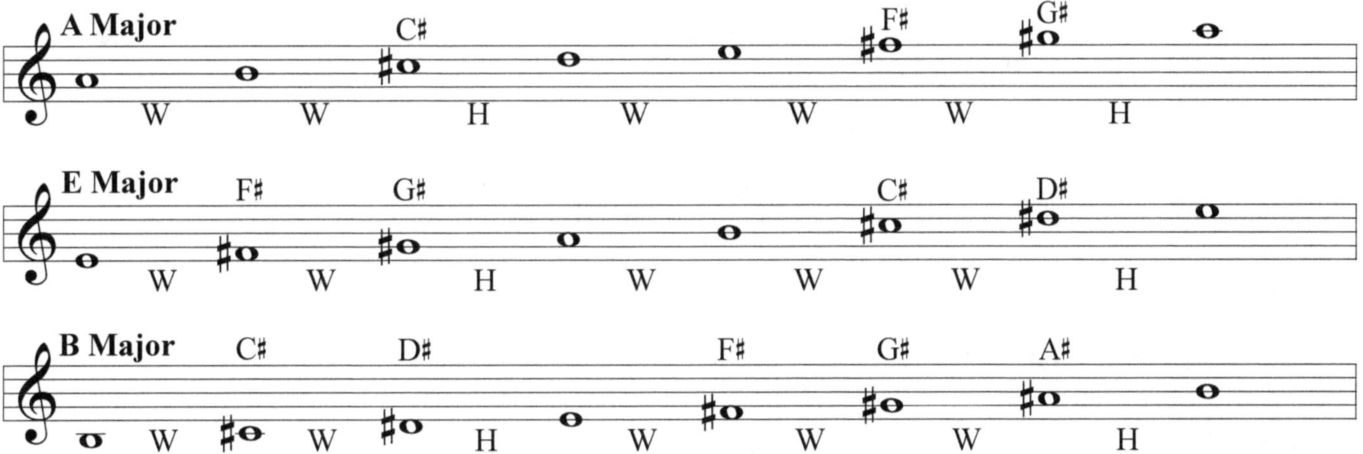

Here are the key signatures for the scales.

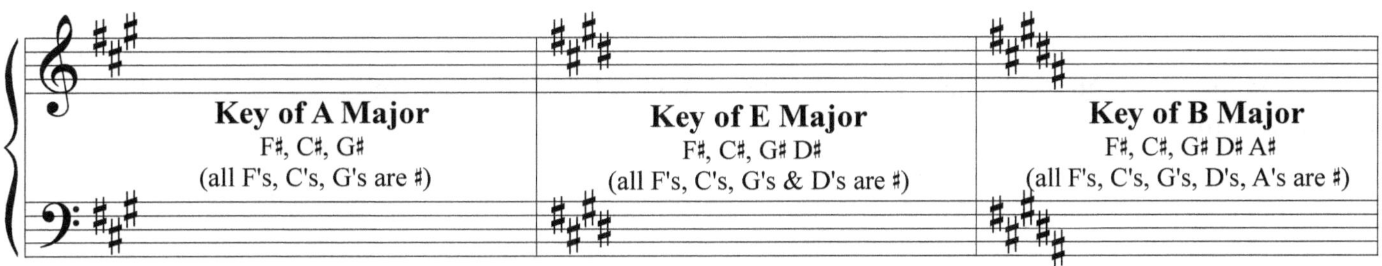

Here is what the scales look like with a key signature. Sharped notes are circled.

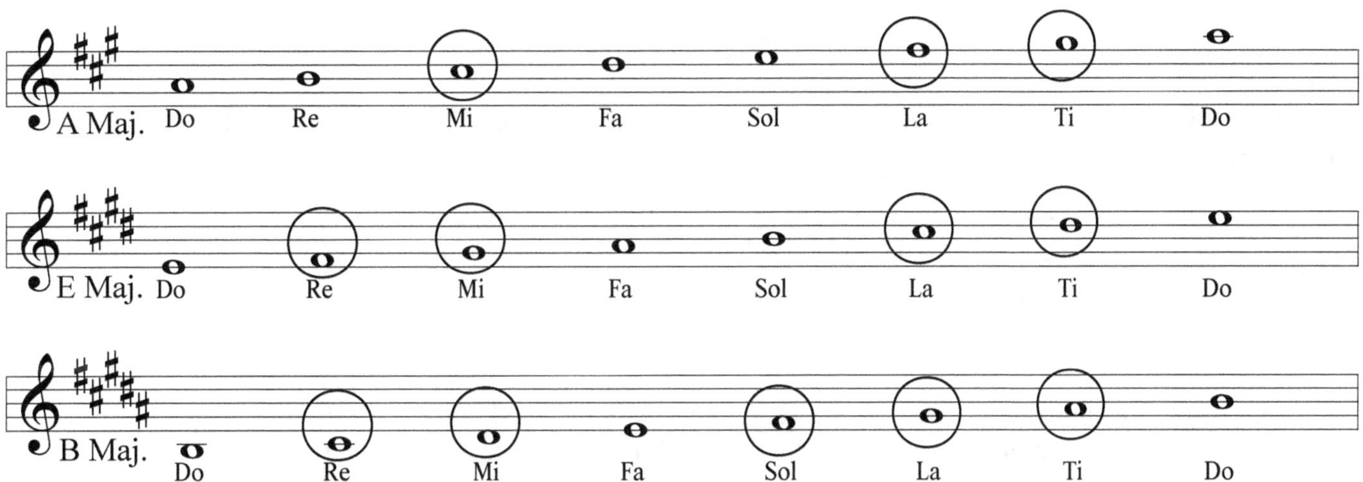

If you don't remember the formula for the Major scale, here are some additional tools for remembering how to identify a key signature.

For sharp keys (key signatures with sharps), there are two easy ways to identify a key signature.

1. Look at the last sharp (farthest one to the right), then name the next note in the musical alphabet. That's the key! In A Major, for example, the farthest sharp to the right is G♯. The next letter in the musical alphabet is A, so the key is A Major.

2. Look at the last sharp (farthest to the right), and it is the "Ti" in the Major scale. If the last sharp (farthest to the right) is "Ti" then "Do" is the next note. In the key of E Major, D♯ is the last sharp in the key signature, so it is "Ti." If D♯ is "Ti" then E is "Do." The key is E Major.

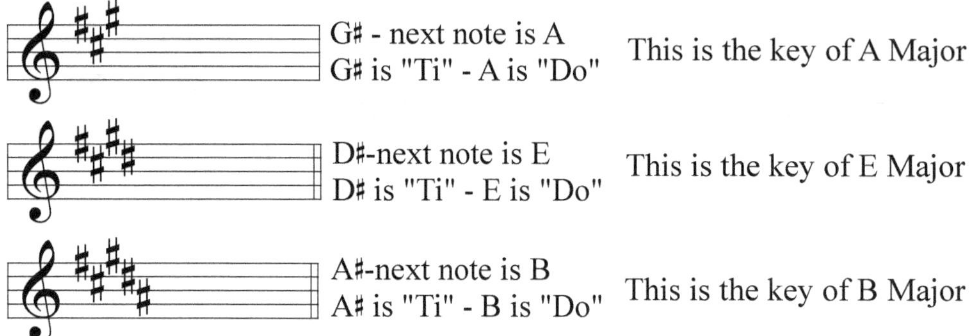

The 2 key signatures with sharps that were introduced in Level 1 are the keys of G & D, in which the same rules to find the key signature apply.

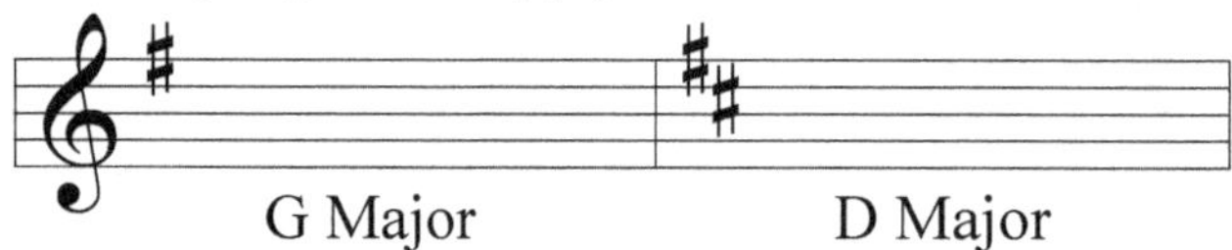

C Major & F Major were also introduced in Level 1. C Major has no ♯/♭, while F Major has one ♭.

For flat keys, you can use the following tool to determine the key.

1. Look at the last flat, it is the "Fa" of the Major scale. From there, you can count up to "Do" to figure out the key.

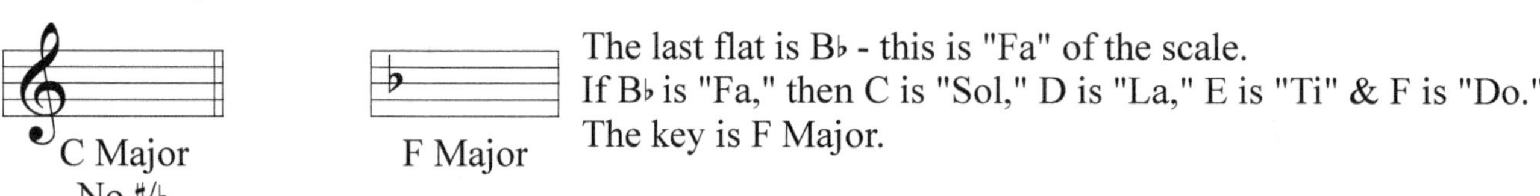

*When sharps or flats appear in a key signature, <u>all</u> sharped or flatted notes are affected; they do not have to be on the same line or space that the sharp and flat are on in the key signature.

For instance, in the key of G Major, <u>all</u> F's are F♯'s, not just the F on the top line of the Treble staff and the 4th line of the Bass staff.

Review: Lesson 5

1. Circle the correct pattern of Whole steps and Half steps that create a Major scale.

   a. W H W W W H W

   b. W W H W W W H

2. Add the necessary ♯ or ♭ to the scales below to create Major scales. Make sure you draw the ♯/♭ before the note that is affected. The center part of the flat and sharp must be on the same line/space of the note it is affecting.

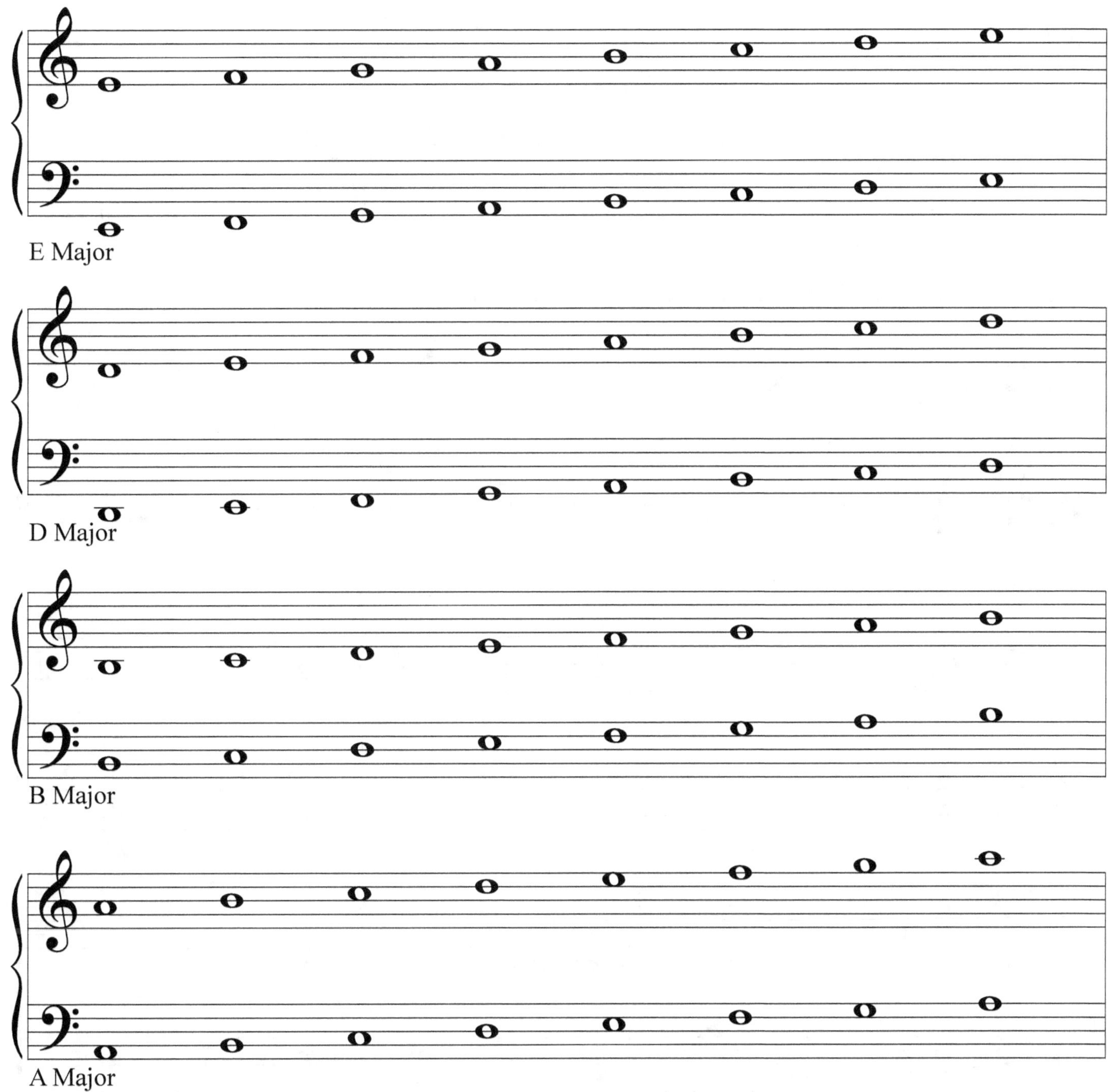

3. Name the Major key for each of these key signatures. The first one is done for you.

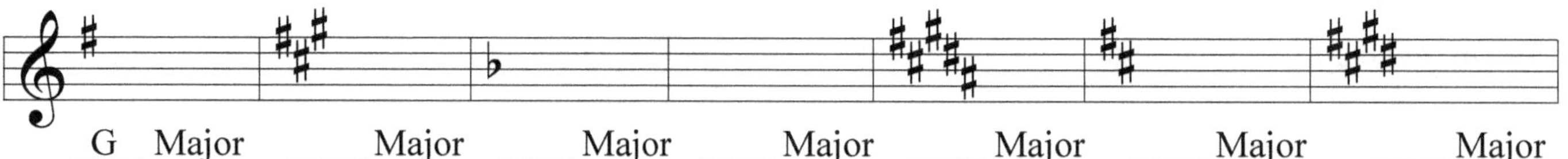

4. Draw the key signature in both the Treble and Bass staves for each of the requested keys. Make sure you add the ♯/♭ to the correct line/space and keep the center part of the ♯/♭ on the correct line/space. Look at question 3 for hints.

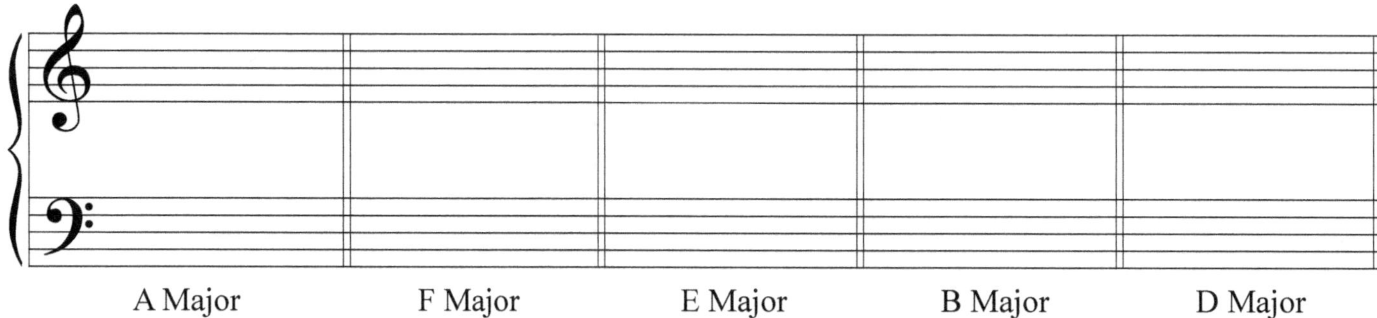

5. Circle the notes affected by the key signature. Pay attention to clef changes.

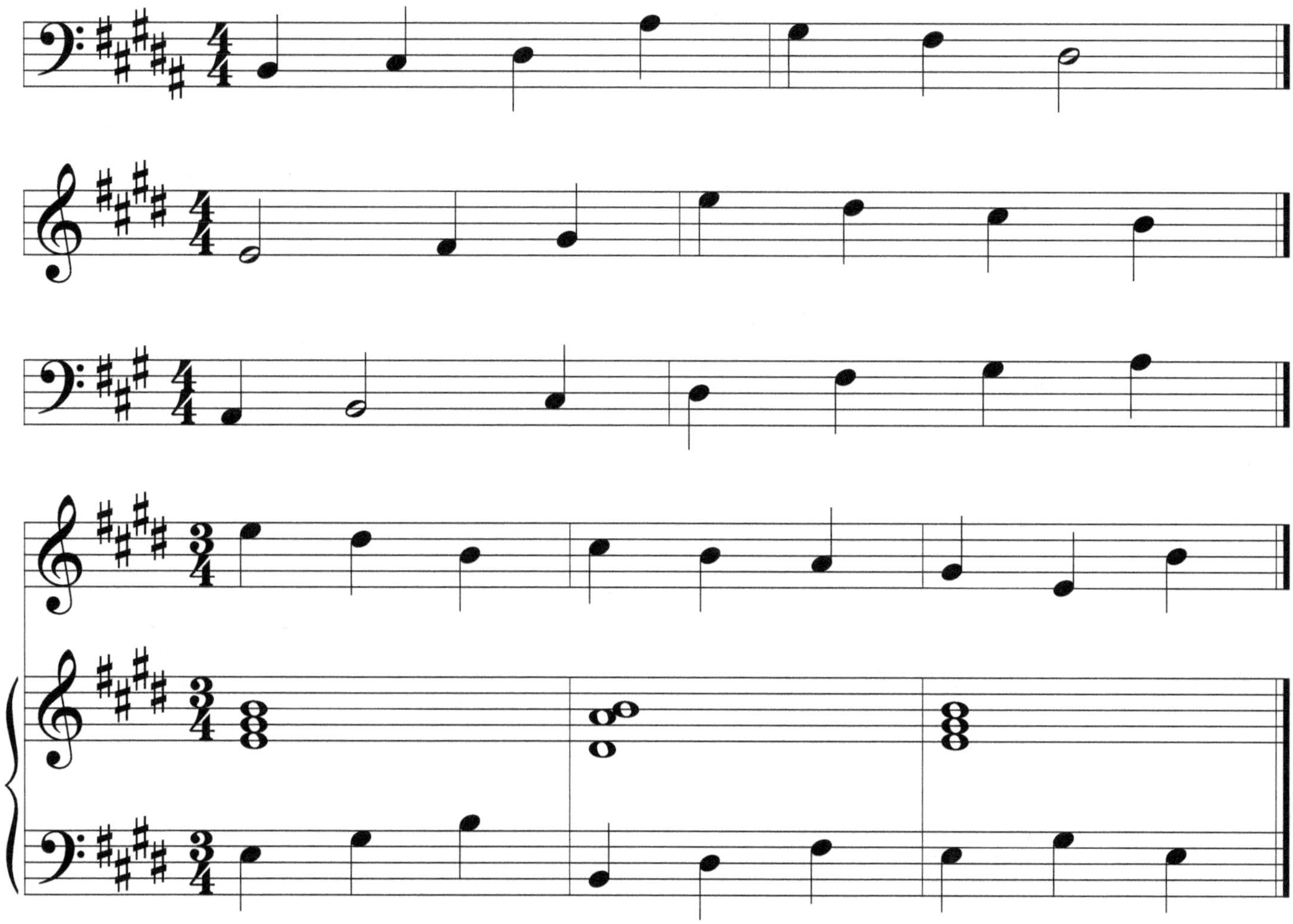

Review: Lessons 1-5

1. Circle "Tie" or "Slur" for the examples below.

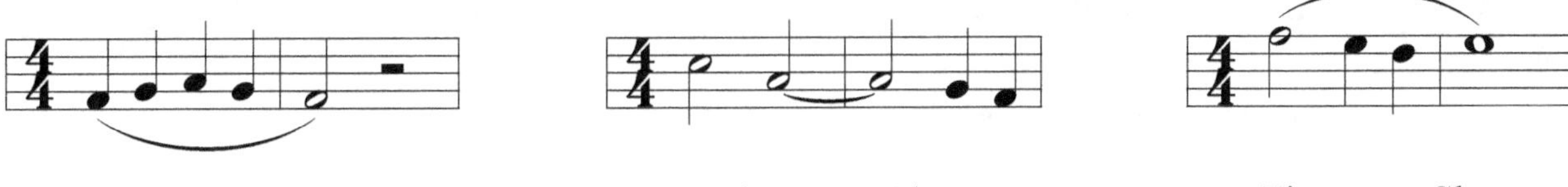

Tie - Slur　　　Tie - Slur　　　Tie - Slur

2. Check how many beats these tied notes receive in 4/4 time.

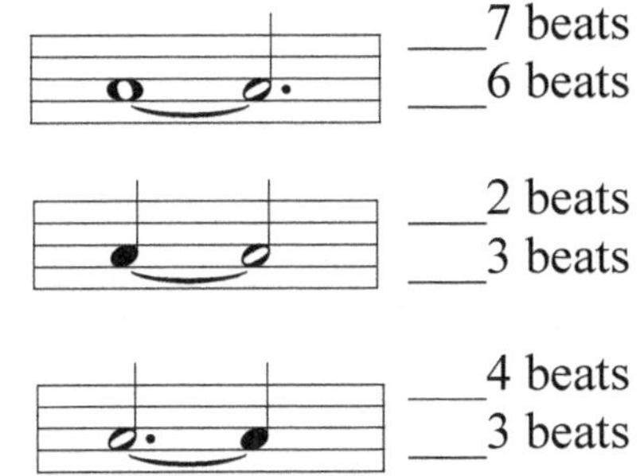

3. Add a **slur** over or under the notes in measures 1-2 and measures 3-4 in the examples below.
Remember to connect the slurs to the note head, not the stem.

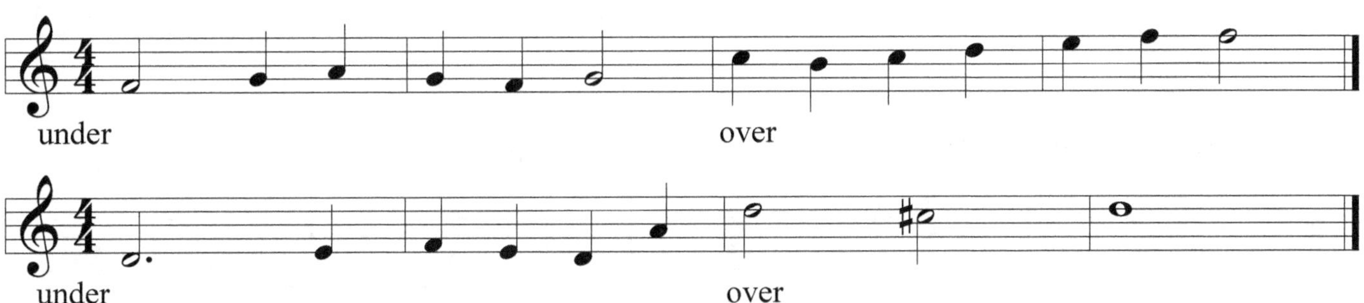

4. Add a **tie** between the 2 notes in the measures indicated by the arrows. Remember to connect the tie to the note head, not the stem.

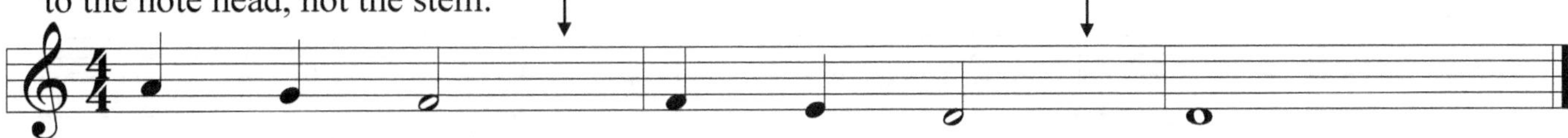

5. Look at the following example, then write out how it would be sung on the blank staff below.

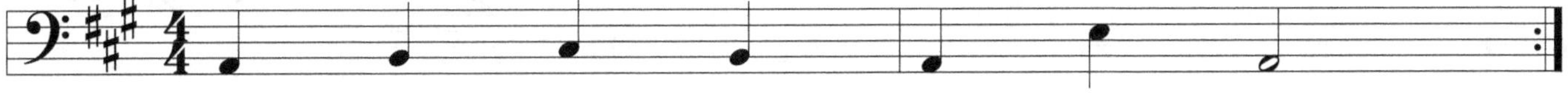

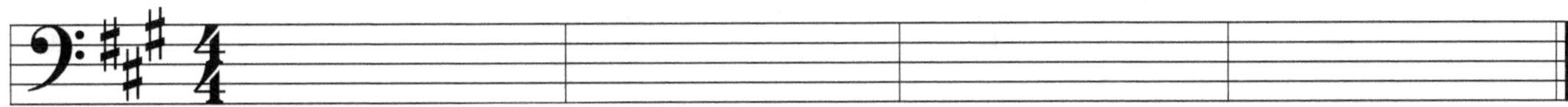

6. Answer the questions about this musical example. Check your answers.

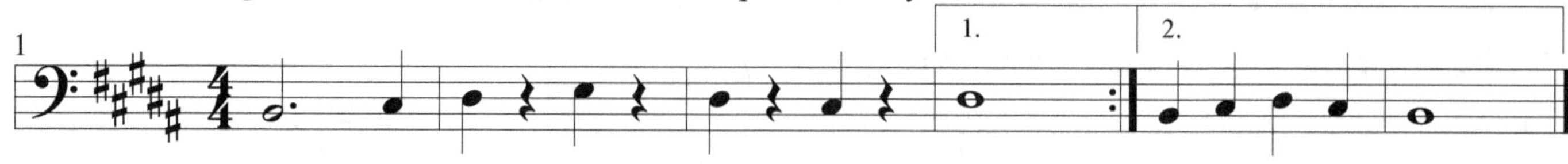

a. What measure comes after measure 4? ____5
____1

b. What is the order of measures for how you would sing this?

____1 - 2 - 3 - 4 - 5 - 6
____1 - 2 - 3 - 4 - 1 - 2 - 3 - 5 - 6

7. Check the correct counting for the example below.

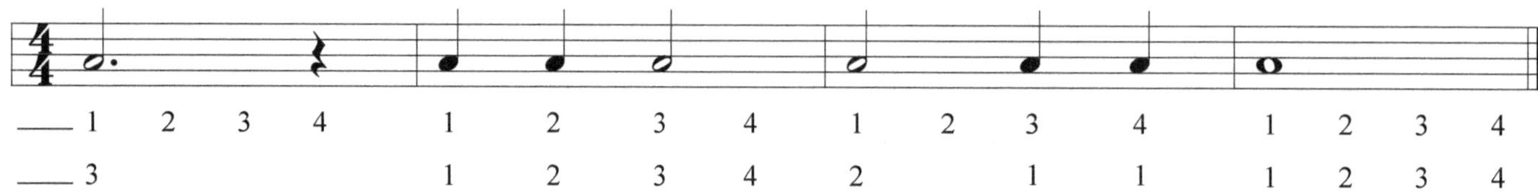

8. Write the beats under each note/rest in the following example.

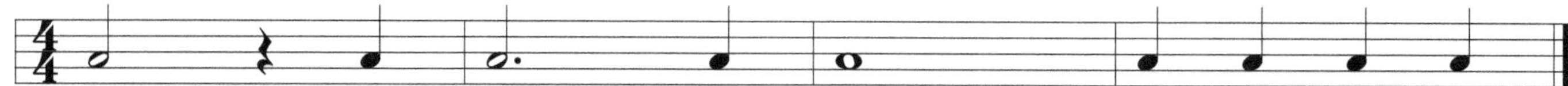

9. Add the 3 missing bar lines and a double bar line to the example below.

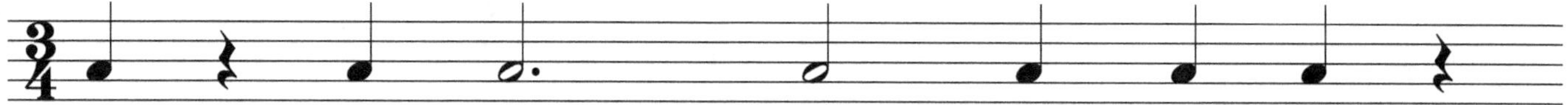

10. Add **one** missing note or rest to complete each measure in the example below.

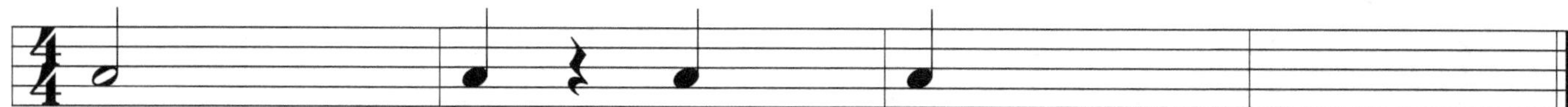

11. Write the letter name of each note.

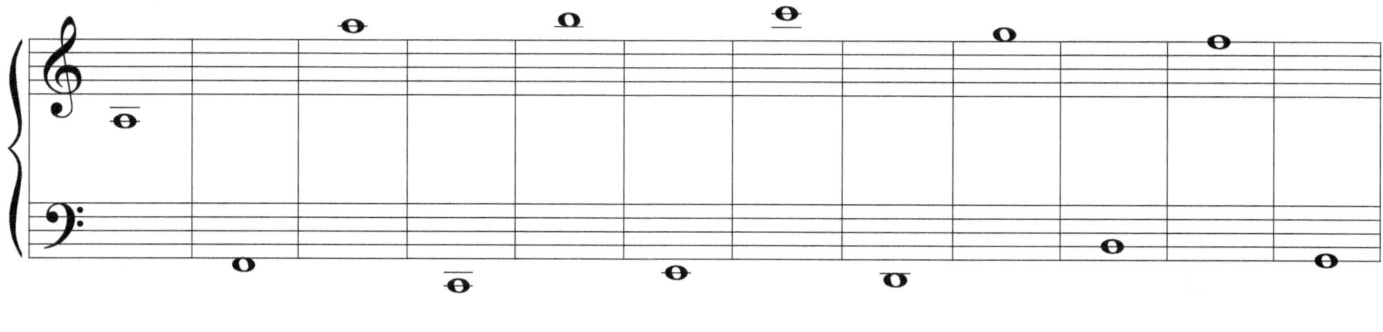

____ ____ ____ ____ ____ ____ ____ ____ ____ ____ ____ ____

12. Add the necessary ♯ or ♭ to the scales below to create Major scales.

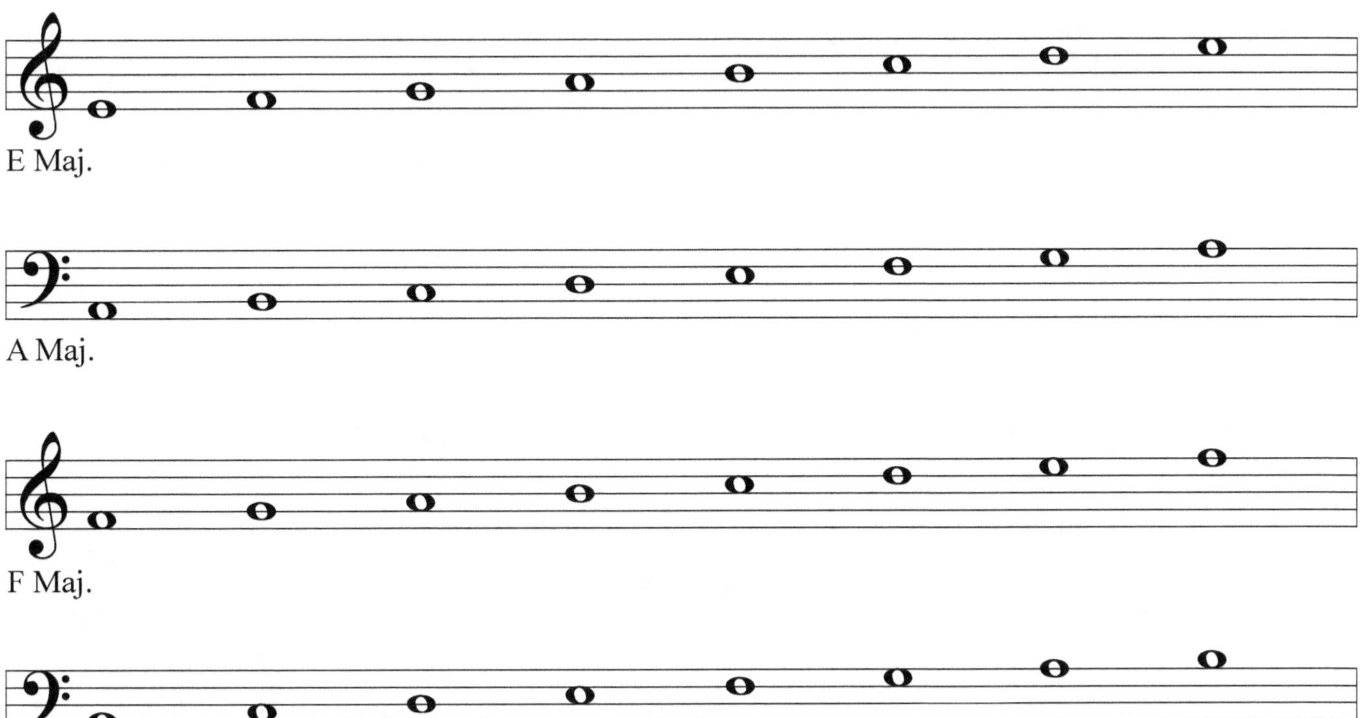

13. Name the Major key for each of these key signatures.

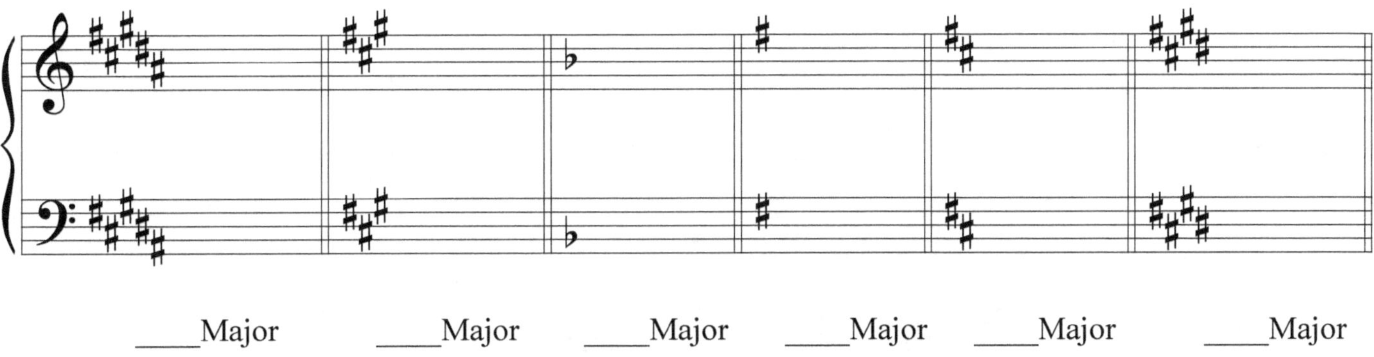

____Major ____Major ____Major ____Major ____Major ____Major

Lesson 6: Triads

A Triad, or 3-note chord, is formed when the first, third, and fifth notes of a scale are sung or played, either consecutively or at the same time. The root, or the lowest note of a triad, determines its letter name.

Example: A Major. A is the 1st/root, C♯ is the 3rd/middle note, E is the 5th/top note

This is a "root position" chord

The following examples show the Major Scales and Major Triads formed on the first note of the scale (Do). The 1st, 3rd, & 5th notes (Do-Mi-Sol) are circled.

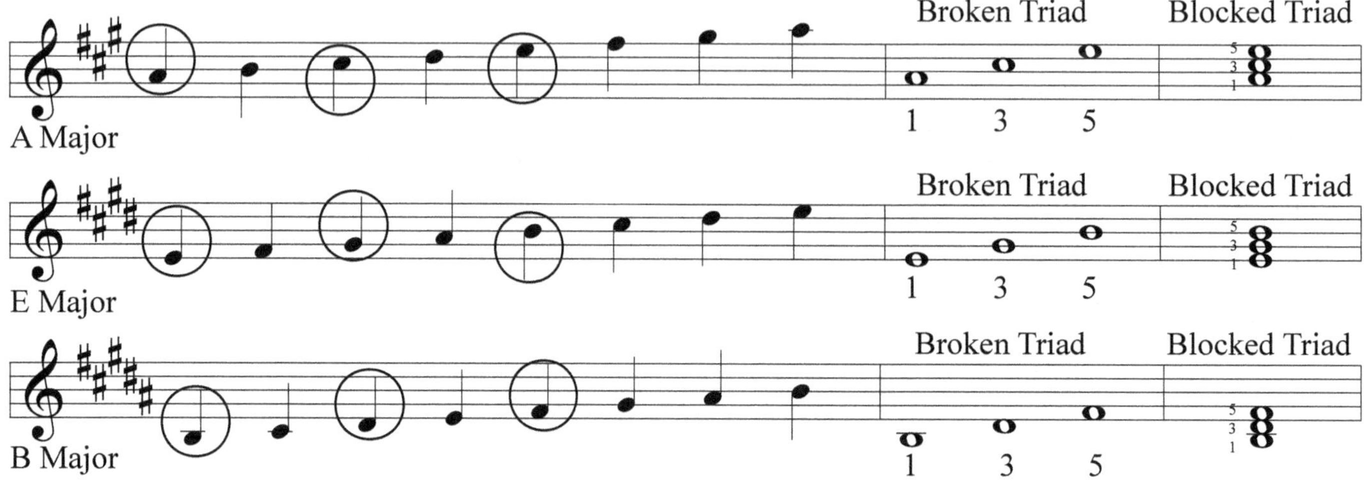

Here are the root position triads in both clefs.

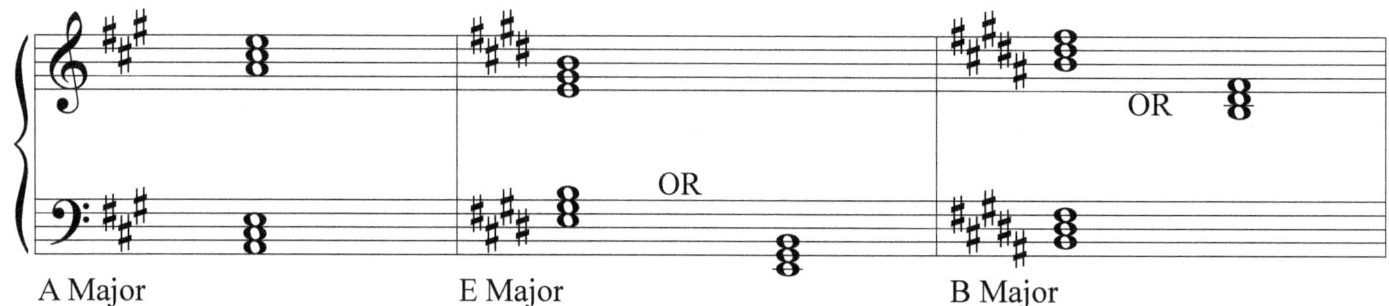

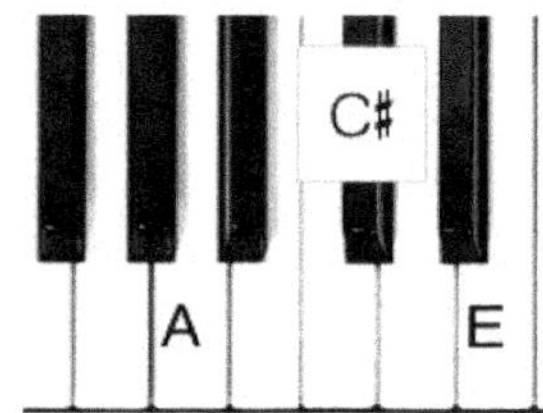

This is what an A Major triad looks like on a piano keyboard.

Review: Lesson 6

1. Name the following triads. Remember, look at the bottom note (root) for the "name" of the triad.

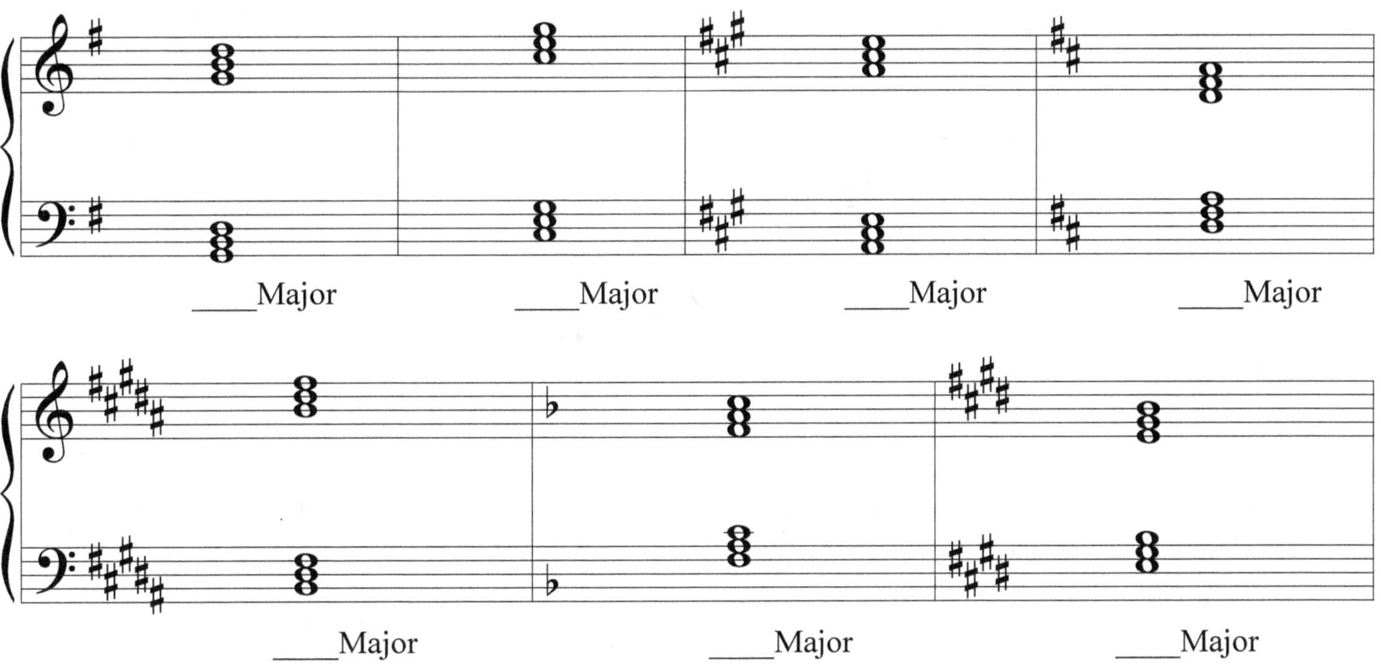

2. For the following examples, <u>draw the correct key signature</u>, then <u>add the root position triads</u> to both the Treble and Bass clefs. Look at question 1 for hints.

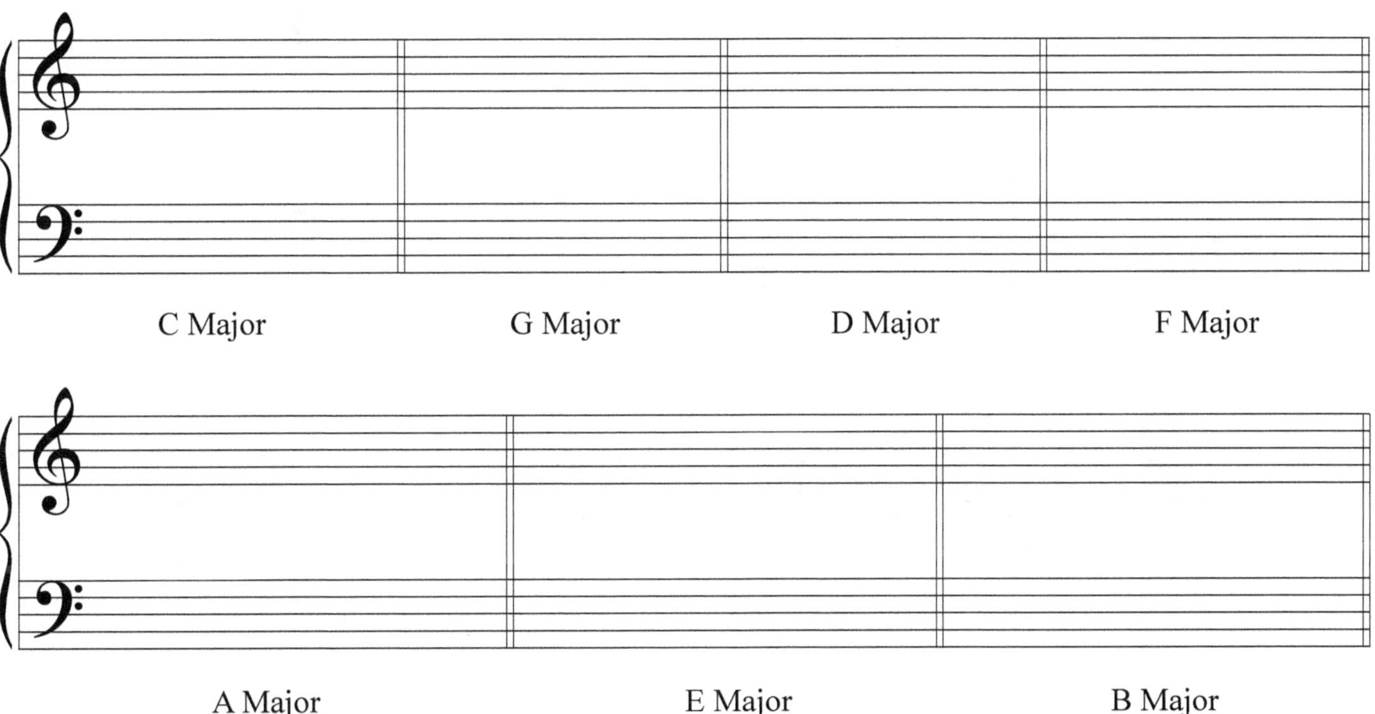

3. Circle the three notes in the scale below that make up a root position triad.

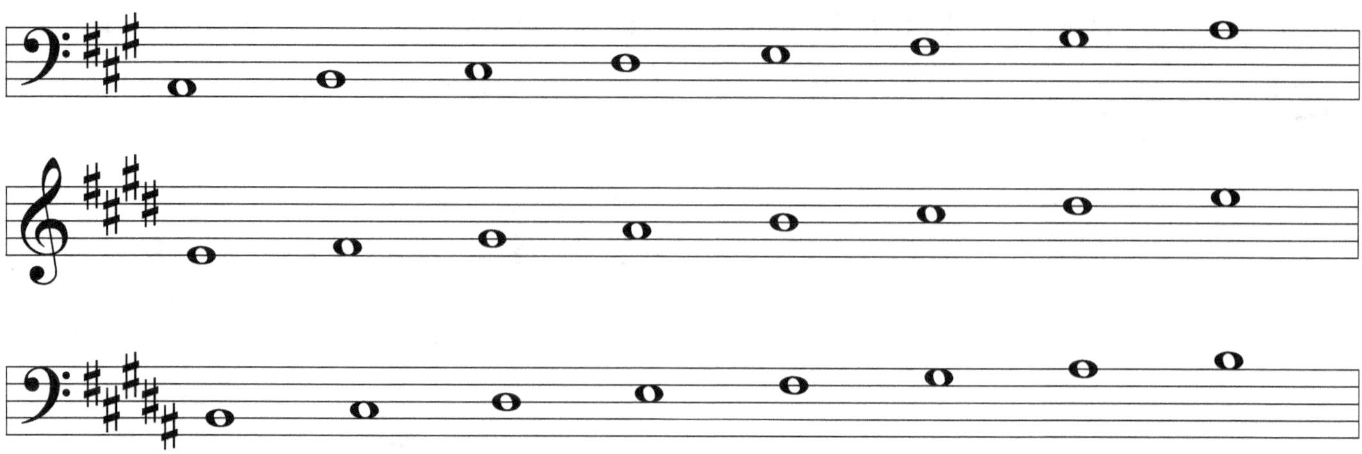

4. Each of these triads should have 3 notes (Do-Mi-Sol/root-middle-top). First, determine the key, then fill in the missing note to create a root position triad for the given key.

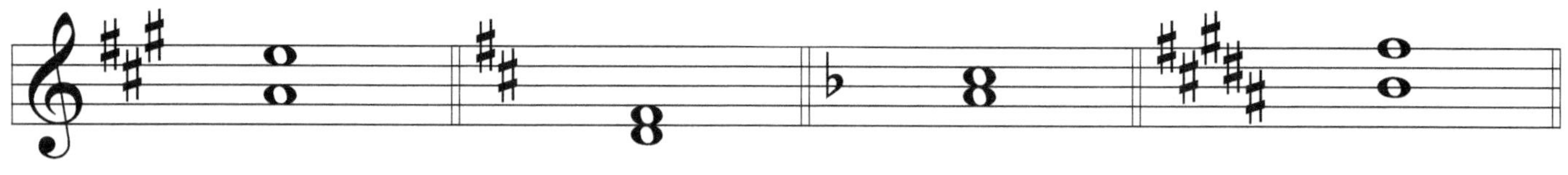

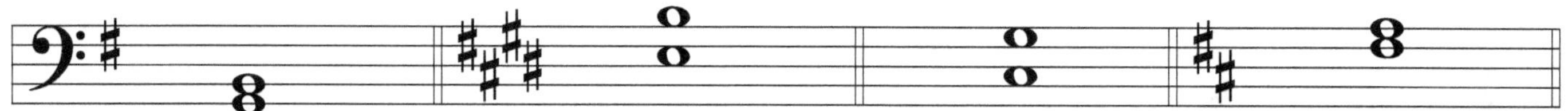

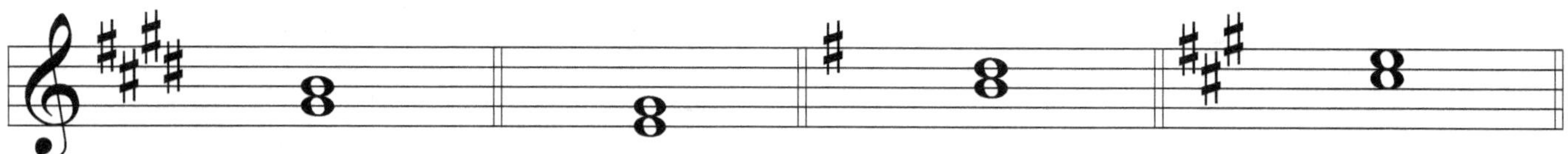

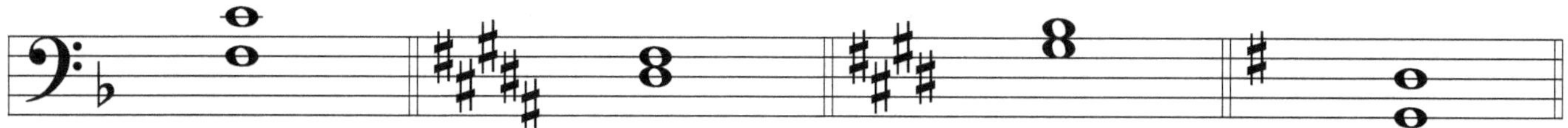

Lesson 7: Intervals (4ths & 5ths)

An Interval, in music, is the distance between any two notes. In this level, the intervals of a 4th and 5th will be covered. The intervals of a 2nd & 3rd were covered in Level 1.
When counting intervals, be sure to include the bottom and top notes.

For singing, Do-Fa is a 4th, Do-Sol is a 5th. Intervals are sung melodically (one note at a time), or harmonically (two notes at the same time - two singers singing at the same time).

Look at the examples below. Notice how the interval of a 4th has a line and a space note. The interval of a 5th either has 2 line notes or 2 space notes.

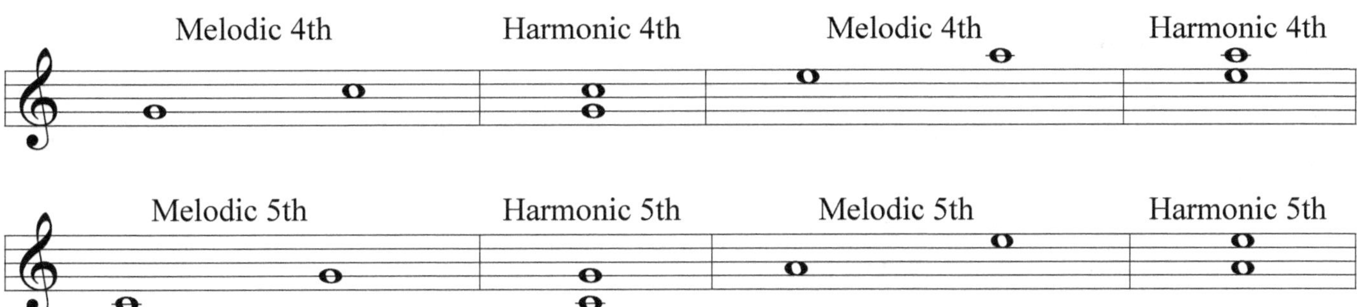

In singing, 2nds, 3rds, 4ths & 5ths use the following solfege.

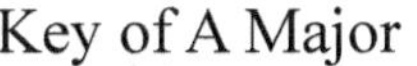

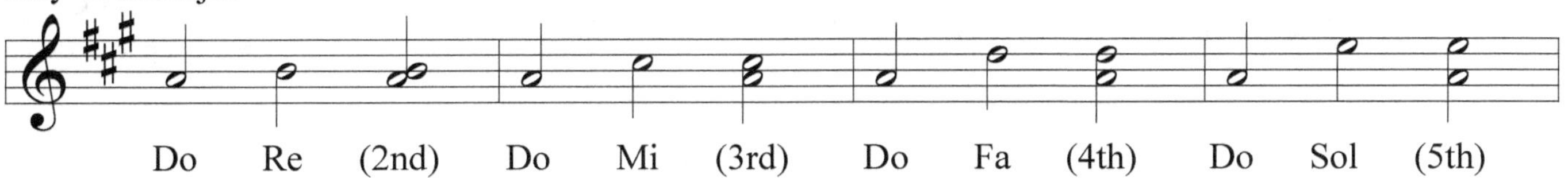

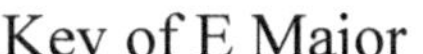

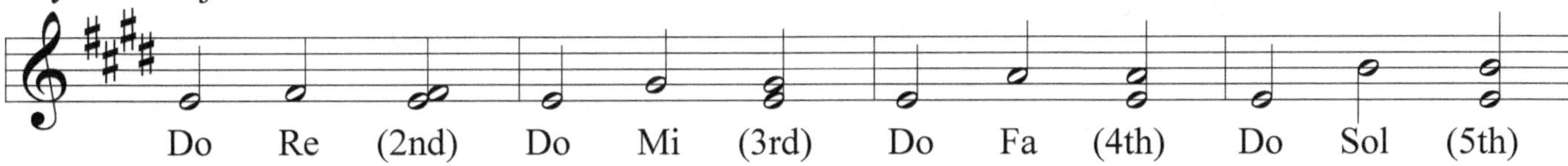

Key of B Major

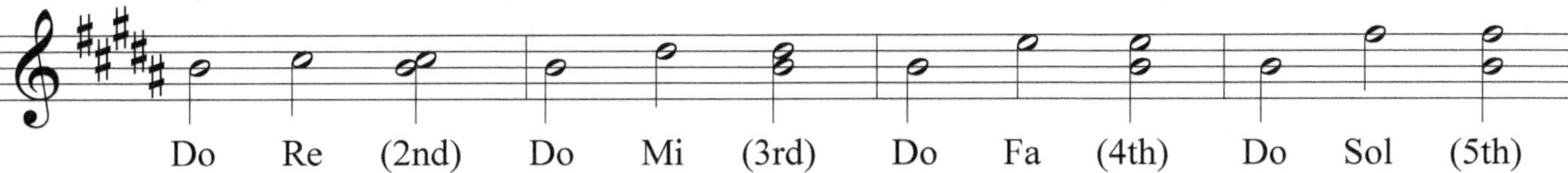

On the piano keyboard below, you can see the distance between the intervals. If you have a piano, keyboard, or piano app, play and sing these notes so you can hear the difference between the intervals.

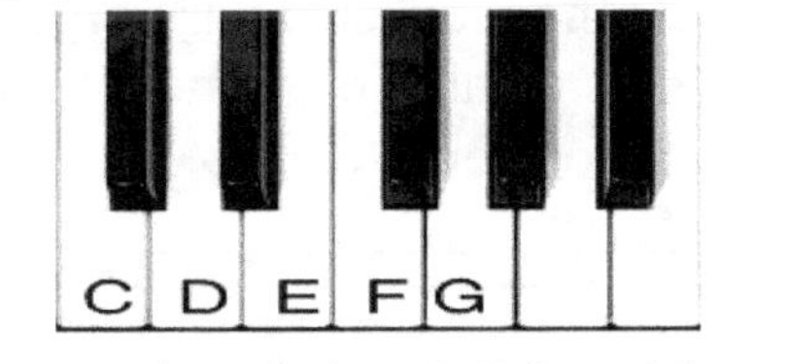

C-D is a 2nd   C-E is a 3rd   C-F is a 4th   C-G is a 5th

Review: Lesson 7

1. Circle all of the harmonic 4ths.

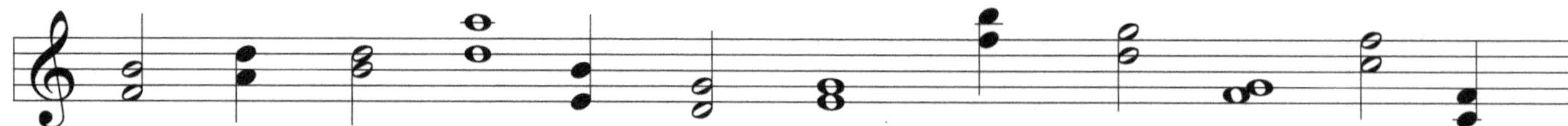

2. Circle all of the harmonic 5ths.

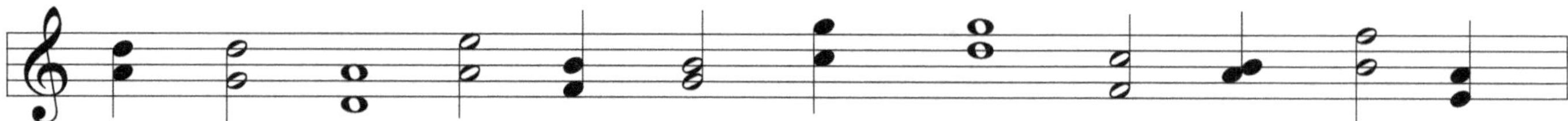

3. Label each melodic interval as a 4th or 5th.

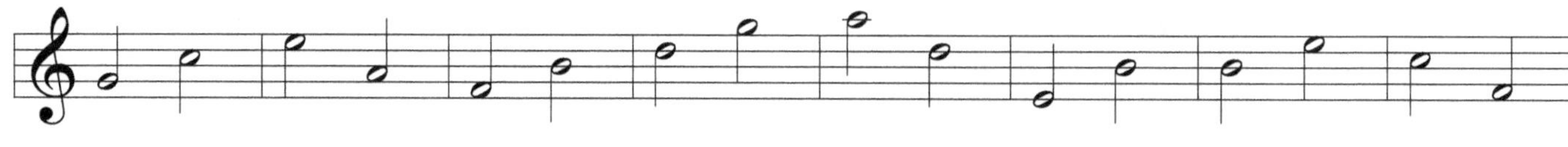

4. Name each interval: 2nd, 3rd, 4th or 5th.

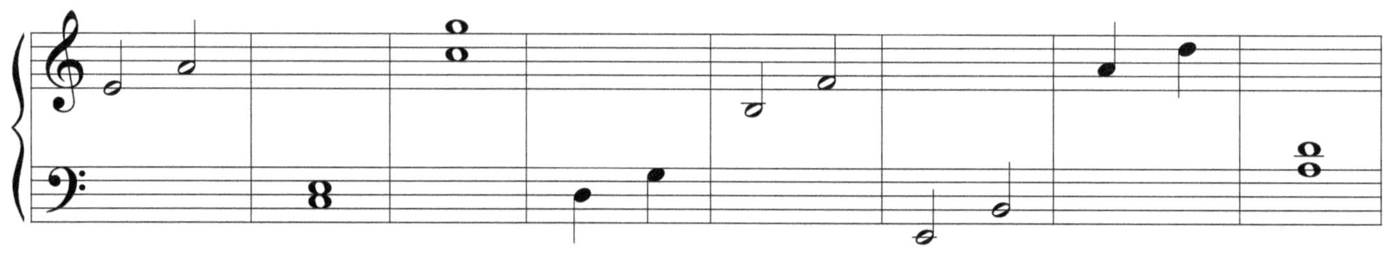

5. Add one note per measure to complete the requested melodic intervals.
Add the note after and above the given note. Make sure you add stems in the correct direction.
Use half notes. The first one is done for you.

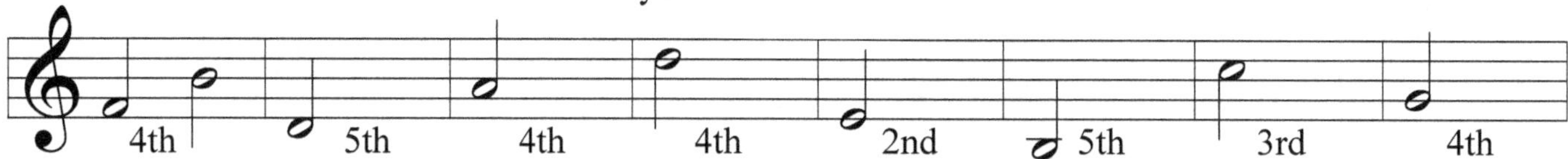

6. Add one note per measure to complete the requested melodic intervals.
Add the note after and below the given note. Make sure you add stems in the correct direction.
Use quarter notes. The first one is done for you.

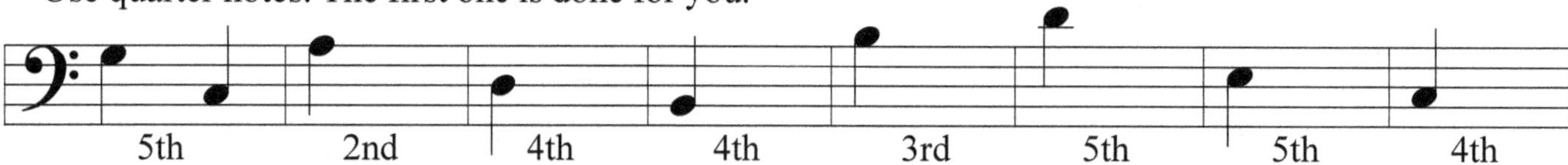

7. Add one note per measure to complete the requested harmonic intervals.
Add the note above the given note. 2nds go above and next to the given note.
Use whole notes. The first one is done for you.

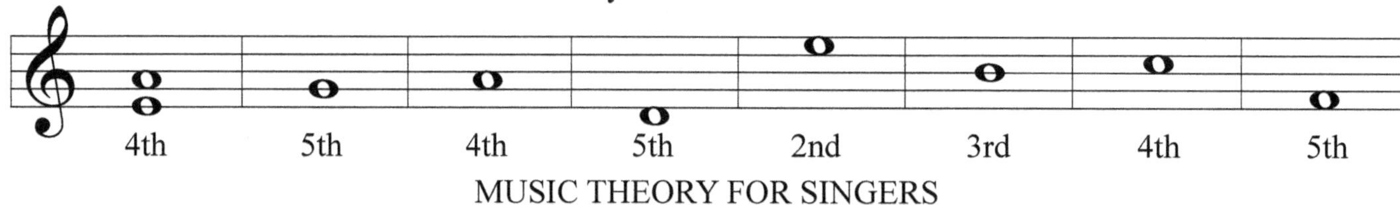

Lesson 8: Vocal Diction & IPA

Every time we sing a song, we are telling a story. As singers, we have to be exceptionally clear with how we pronounce the words of our songs, or our audience will not understand us and our story will not be told.

If you reference a dictionary in any Latin based language (English, Italian, French, German, Spanish, Latin, etc.) you will see some symbols next to the words. These symbols make up the International Phonetic Alphabet, or IPA. The IPA represents the sounds of a language. In fact, the IPA represents nearly any vowel or consonant made by human beings!

In this lesson, we'll focus on a few of the vowel sounds in the IPA. You will learn what the letter looks like in our language, what the IPA symbol for that letter is, and what it sounds like. The IPA symbols from Level 1 will also be in our chart below.

Before we look at the symbols, make a couple of sounds so you can see all of the different positions your tongue moves to in order to make each sound.

Say "ah" as in the word "father," and "ee" as in the word "meet." You'll notice that when you say "ah," your tongue is at the bottom of your mouth, and when you say "ee" the center of your tongue moves to the roof of your mouth, while the tip remains down and behind the bottom teeth. When singing, we must be aware of any tension in our tongue, and ensure that it is in the proper position for creating accurate vowel sounds.

Here is a chart of the vowels we will learn in this lesson, along with their english equivalent.

IPA SYMBOL	SOUND IN ENGLISH WORD	IPA SPELLING OF WORD	TONGUE/LIPS PLACEMENT
i	ski	[ski]	Center of tongue is high Lips relaxed
ɛ	led	[lɛd]	Low tongue Lips relaxed
ɑ	father	[ˈfɑðər]	Low tongue Lips relaxed
o	obey	[oʊˈbeɪ]	Low tongue, tip behind bottom teeth Rounded lips
u	goose	[gus]	Low tongue, tip behind bottom teeth Rounded lips
ɪ	kit	[kɪt]	High tongue, sides touching top teeth Lips relaxed
e	ate	[eɪt]	High tongue, sides touching top teeth Lips relaxed
ə	afraid	[əˈfreɪd]	Mid tongue, tip behind bottom teeth Lips relaxed

New in Lev. 2

courtesy of Sarah Sandvig

Practice saying the sounds above, and the english words in the second column.

Check that your tongue and lips are in the position described in the last column.

Additional IPA symbols, like the ones you see in the 3rd column will be introduced in later levels of these books.

Review: Lesson 8

1. Check the English word that contains the same sound as the given IPA symbol.

i	___Bit ___Feet	ɑ	___Late ___Rot	u	___Food ___Cup	e	___Bet ___Mate
ɛ	___Mess ___Leap	o	___Float ___Pot	ɪ	___Pit ___Bite	ə	___About ___Best

2. Circle the correct answer for the proper tongue and lip position for each IPA symbol. Say each sound, it will help!

ɪ - Tongue is - high- and lips are - relaxed -
- low - - rounded -

e - Tongue is - high- and lips are - relaxed -
- low - - rounded -

ə - Tongue is - high- and lips are - relaxed -
- low - - rounded -

o - Tongue is - high- and lips are - relaxed -
- low - - rounded -

u - Tongue is - high- and lips are - relaxed -
- low - - rounded -

3. Write a word in the blank provided that uses the given IPA sound. Don't use any of the words from above or on the previous page!

i ________________ ɑ ________________

u ________________ ɛ ________________

o ________________ ɪ ________________

ə ________________ e ________________

Lesson 9: Sight-Singing

In order to learn a song, singers learn to read both rhythmic patterns and notes (melody) on the staff. Singing a melody for the first time is called "sight-singing." Below are some rhythmic examples using the notes introduced so far.

Hint: When singing rhythmic examples, take a breath on the rests: then you won't miss them! *Tap* and *say* the beats, then sing the examples on a La (choose any pitch that suits your voice).

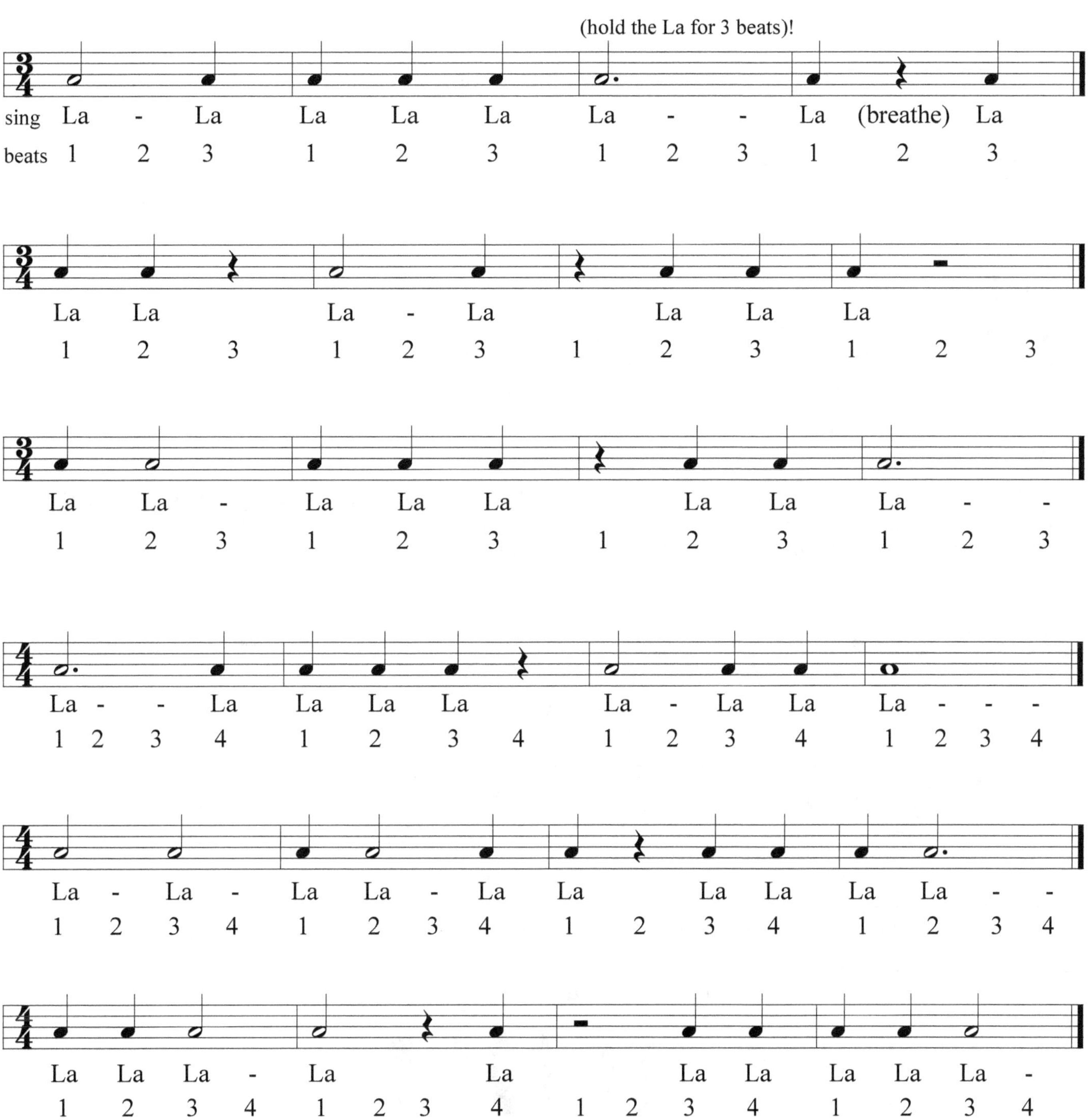

Melody & Solfege

Solfege is a system of assigning a syllable to each note of a scale, just like in the song "Do-Re-Mi" from the musical *The Sound of Music*.

Solfege is a useful tool when sight-singing. Moveable “Do” is when “Do” matches the **root** of whatever key you’re in. The following examples contain a Major scale in the three keys covered in this level.

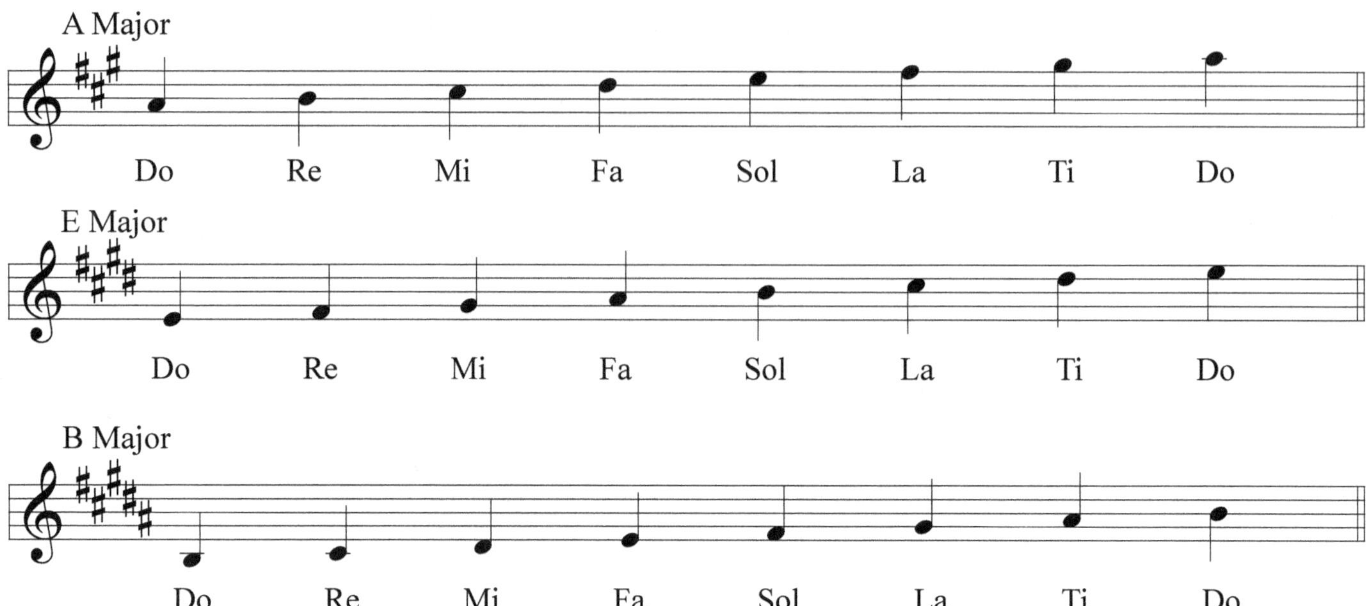

In this Level, you’ll learn to sing melodies with Do, Re, Mi & Fa. The following melodies have the solfege written under the notes for you. Pay attention to the key signature changes. Use the picture of the piano below to find your starting note on your piano or piano app.

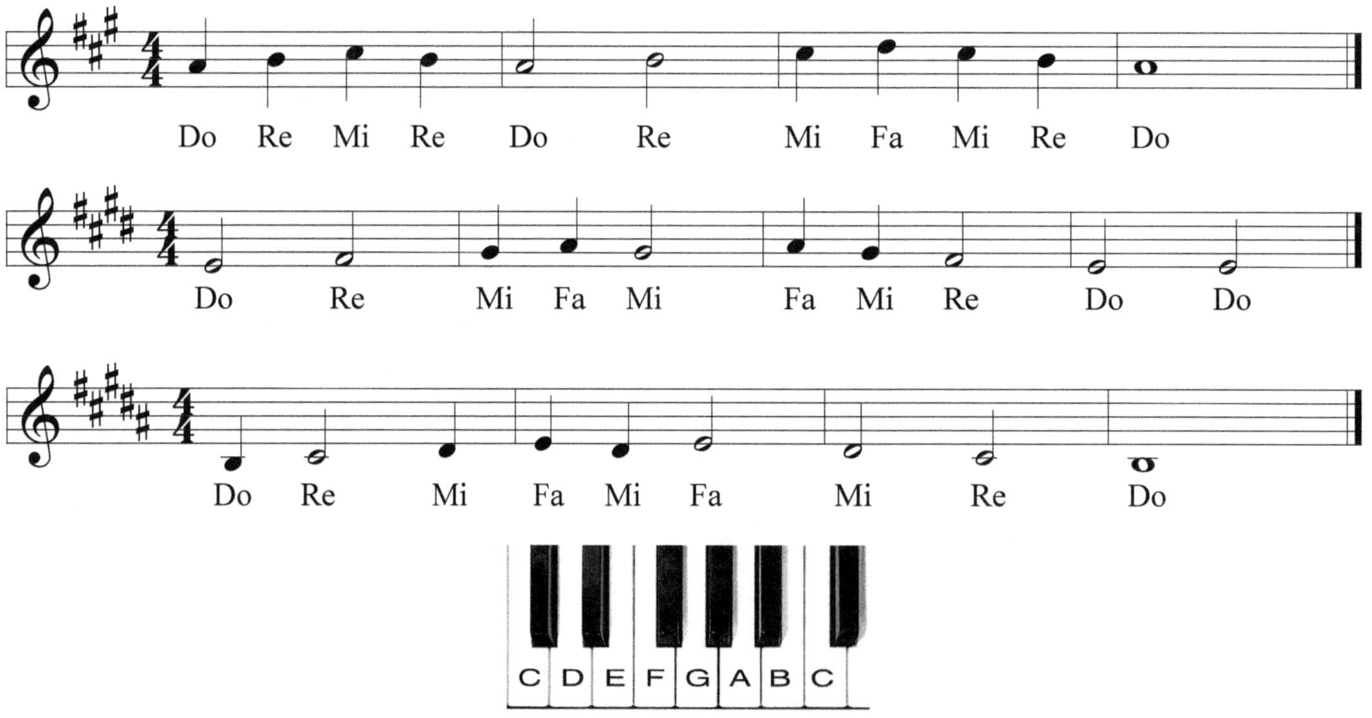

Review: Lesson 9

1. For the following melodies, write the note names, solfege & beats underneath the notes. Practice singing the examples when you are done!

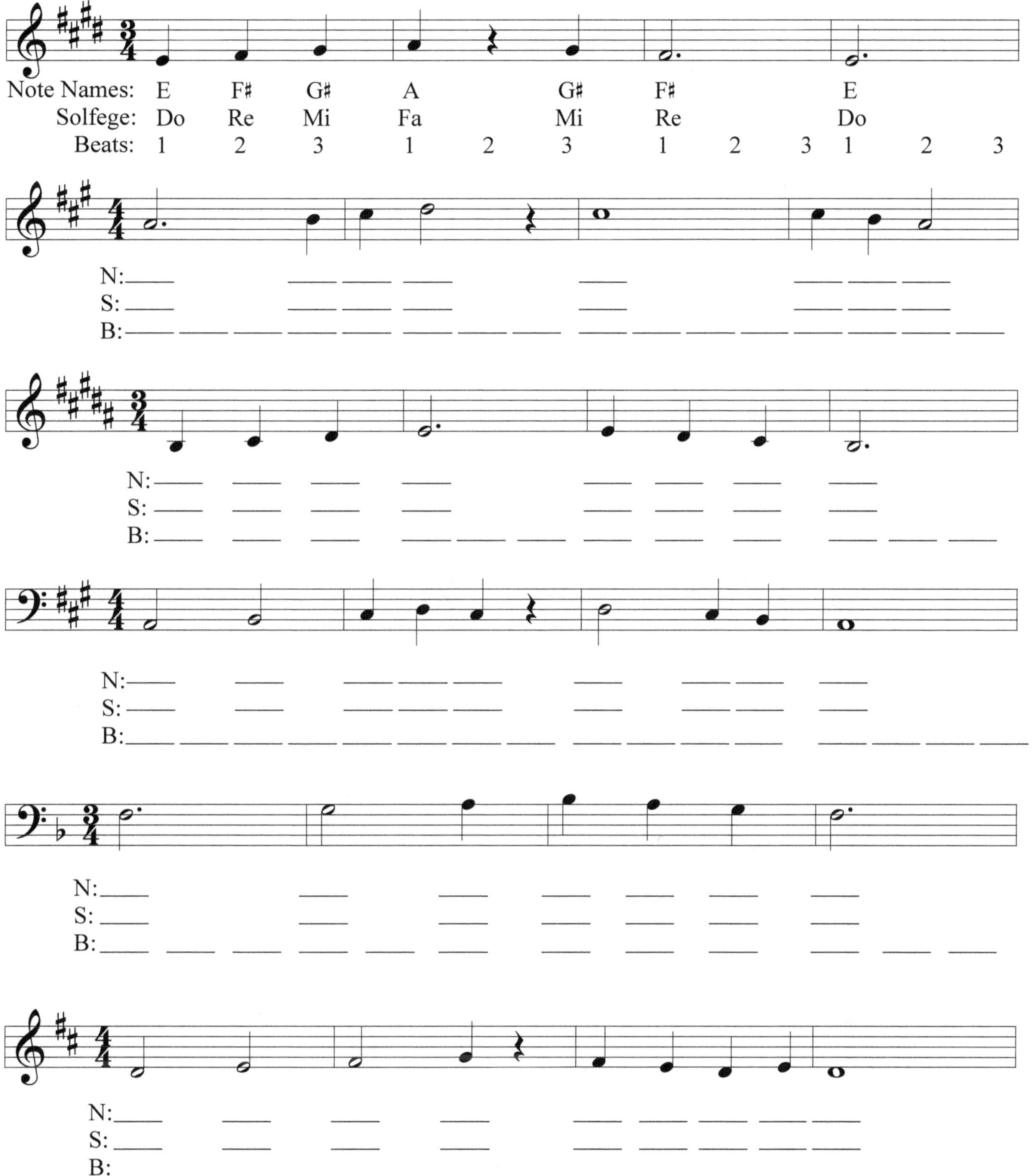

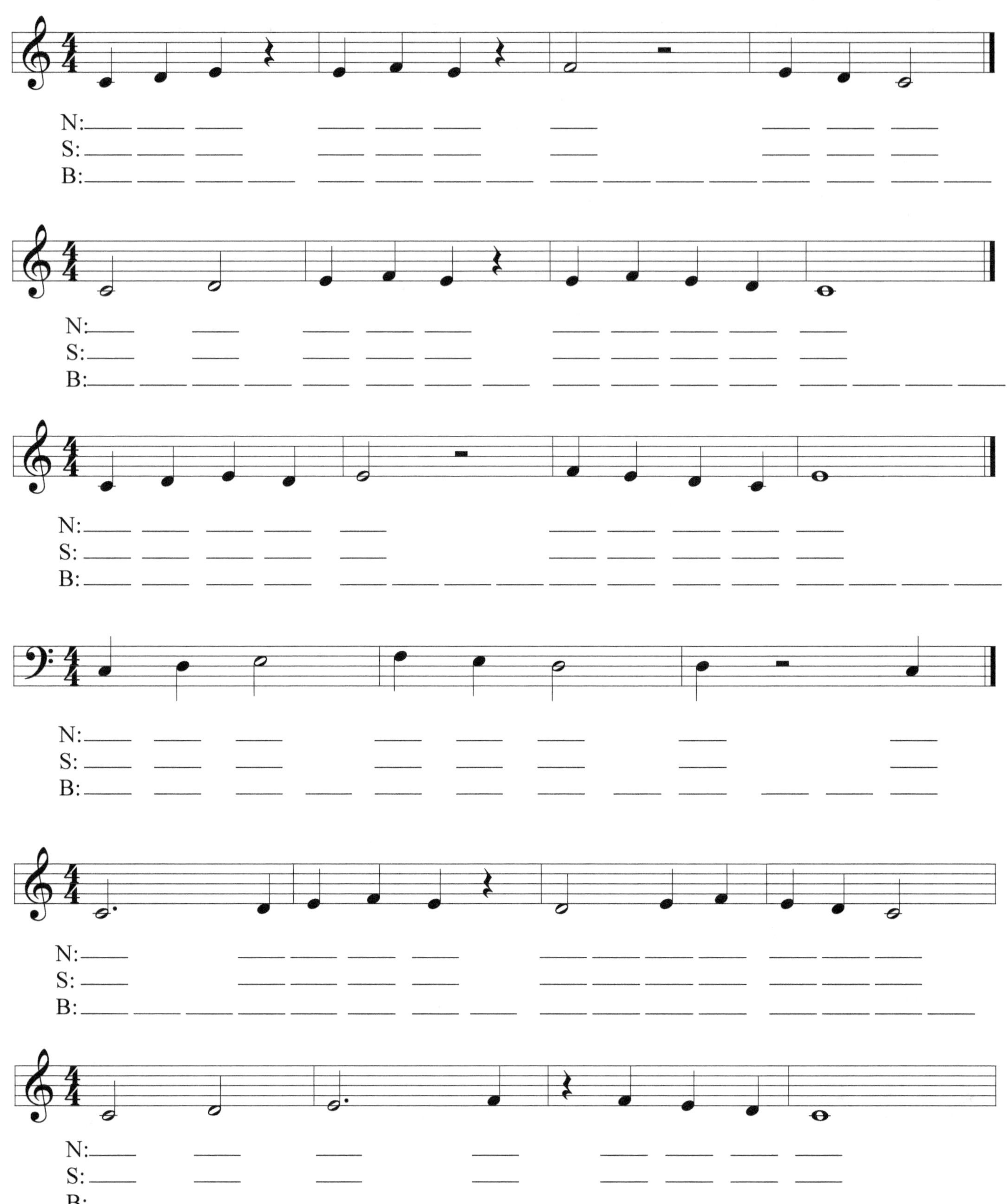
N:
S:
B:
N:
S:
B:
N:
S:
B:
N:
S:
B:
N:
S:
B:
N:
S:
B:

Lesson 10: Musical Terms

A crucial part of understanding music is being able to recognize and define musical terms. Below is a list of terms covered in this level.

a tempo - return to the original tempo

Baroque Period of Music - a term borrowed from architecture to describe Western European music written from approximately 1600 to 1750

crescendo (<) - gradually getting louder

decrescendo (>) - gradually getting softer

dot (·) - added to a note or rest, it increases the length of the note or rest by 1/2 of its original value

fortissimo (*ff*) - very loud

IPA- the International Phonetic Alphabet: a standard representation of the sounds of spoken language

ledger lines - short lines added above or below the staff so that notes can be written there

mezzo forte (*mf*) - medium loud

mezzo piano (*mp*) - medium soft

pianissimo (*pp*) - very soft

Renaissance Period of Music - in musical history, the period between approximately 1425 and 1600

repeat signs - two dots placed before or after a double bar line, indicating a repeat of the music between the signs

ritardando (rit.) - becoming gradually slower

slur - a curved line connecting two or more different notes, indicating smoothness

tenuto (ten.) - sustain a note for its full value

tie - a curved line connecting two notes of the same pitch, which combines their values

Review: Lesson 10

1. Check the appropriate answer for each of the following questions.

a. What is a curved line connecting two or more different notes, indicating smoothness.

____tie

____slur

b. Which term means very soft?

____pianissimo

____fortissimo

c. The Renaissance Period of Music was between which years in musical history?

____1425-1600

____1600-1750

d. These signs are placed before or after a double bar line, indicating to sing the music again.

____slurs

____repeat signs

e. This term means to sustain a note for its full value.

____a tempo

____tenuto

f. Which key signature has 4 sharps?

____A Major

____E Major

g. What word has the sound of the IPA symbol "ɪ"?

____fight

____fit

h. Which term means to gradually become slower?

____ritardando

____a tempo

i. Which term means "medium loud?"

____fortissimo

____mezzo forte

j. What is a curved line connecting two notes of the same pitch, which combines their values?

____tie

____slur

2. Complete the following crossword puzzle using the terms from this level.

Level 2 Crossword

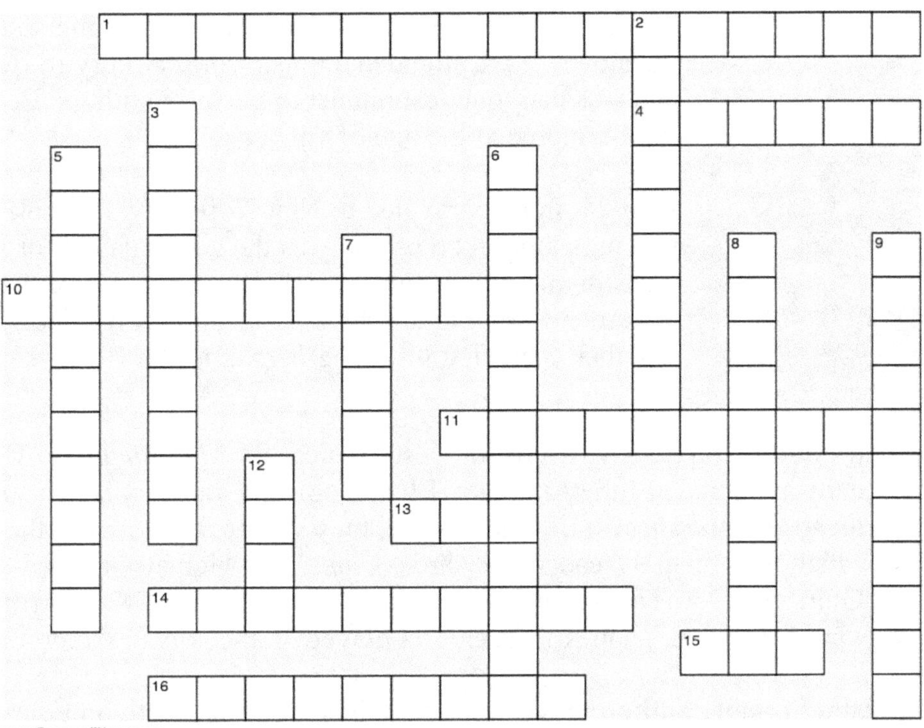

ACROSS

1 in musical history, the period between 1425 and 1600
4 return to the original tempo
10 gradually getting softer
11 medium loud
13 a curved line connecting two notes of the same pitch, which combines their values
14 very loud
15 added to a note, it increases the length of the note by 1/2 of its original value
16 gradually getting louder

DOWN

2 very soft
3 becoming gradually slower
5 two dots placed before or after a double bar line, indicating a repeat of the music between the signs
6 a term borrowed from architecture to describe Western European music written from 1600 to 1750
7 sustain a note for its full value
8 medium soft
9 short lines added above or below the staff so that notes can be written there
12 a curved line connecting two or more different notes, indicating smoothness

crossword created at:
www.CrosswordWeaver.com

Lesson 11: Spotlight on Composers

An important part of music education is learning about the history of music. Studying composers allows for understanding the music we sing and why it was written the way it was. In this level you will learn about Frederick Loewe and Irving Berlin.

FREDERICK LOEWE

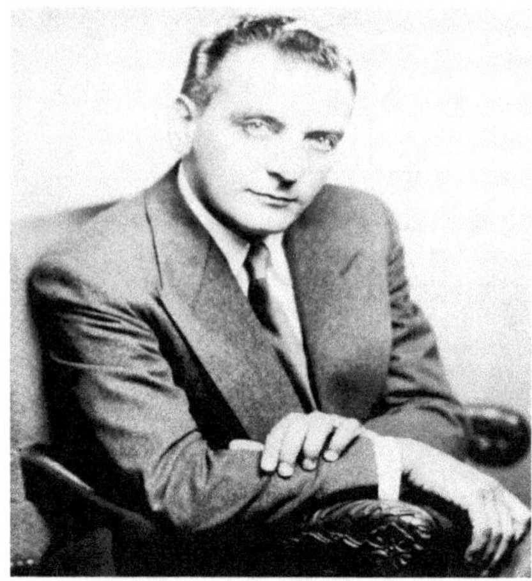
Bettmann/Contributor/Getty

Frederick Loewe was born in the Contemporary period of music on June 10, 1901 in Berlin, Germany. He taught himself to play piano by ear and was composing songs by the age of 7. He attended a music conservatory in Berlin and was the youngest pianist to perform with the Berlin Philharmonic at the age of 13.

In 1924, Loewe traveled to New York City. He took jobs playing piano in clubs and was the accompanist for silent films in movie theaters. In 1942, he met the librettist Alan J. Lerner. Lerner and Loewe wrote several musicals together, their first hit being *Brigadoon* in 1947.

In 1957, Lerner and Loewe won a Tony Award for Best Musical for *My Fair Lady*. The original cast on Broadway included Julie Andrews (Eliza Doolittle) and Rex Harrison (Henry Higgins). Because of the success of this musical, they were asked to write the film musical *Gigi* which won them 9 Academy Awards. *Camelot,* which also starred Julie Andrews as "Guinevere," was also a success. Richard Burton played "King Arthur" (winning a Tony award for the role) and Robert Goulet played "Lancelot" in the production.

Loewe retired to Palm Springs, California where he remained until his death on February 14, 1988.

Best Known Scores and Songs:

Brigadoon *- 1947 (Broadway Musical)- 1954 (Movie)*
"Almost Like Being in Love," "Waitin' For My Dearie," "There But For You Go I"
My Fair Lady *- 1956 (Broadway Musical) - 1964 (Movie)*
" Wouldn't it be Loverly," "I Could have Danced all Night," "Show Me,"
"On the Street Where you Live"
Camelot *- 1960 (Broadway Musical) - 1967 (Movie)*
"If Ever I would Leave You," "C'est Moi," "Camelot," "I Loved You Once in Silence"
"The Simple Joys of Maidenhood"

IRVING BERLIN

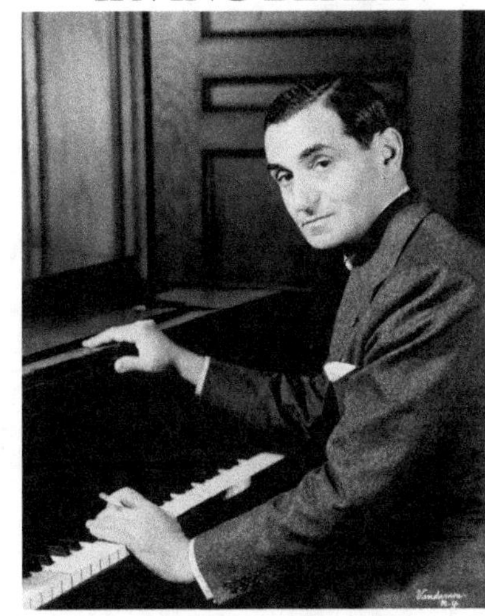
John Springer Collection/Contributor/Getty

Irving Berlin was born in the Contemporary period of music, on May 11, 1888 in Russia. When Berlin was only five years old, he and his family fled to New York. When Berlin was eight, his father passed away and he was forced to drop out of school and work to support his family.

He took some jobs singing in saloons and was a singing waiter. In 1909, Berlin got a job as a staff lyricist with the Ted Snyder Company. In 1911, his song "Alexander's Ragtime Band" became a world-famous hit. This song started a national dance craze.

In 1912, Berlin married Dorothy Goetz, but she died six months later. He wrote his first ballad "When I Lost You" to express his grief. By 1918, Berlin had written several hits including "I Love a Piano," and "A Pretty Girl is Like a Melody." The latter was written for the famous Ziegfeld *Follies of 1919.*

One of Berlin's most famous songs was "God Bless America" which premiered in 1938. This song remains famous to this day. In 1946, Berlin wrote the music and lyrics to the musical *Annie Get Your Gun.* His songs were also featured in the movies *Holiday Inn, The Jazz Singer, Blue Skies* and *Easter Parade.* Berlin fell in love with Ellin Mackay in 1920, and they were married a few years later. They were married for 63 years and had four children. Irving Berlin wrote over 1,500 songs before he was 30 and wrote scores for 19 Broadway shows and 18 movies. He was 101 when he died on September 22, 1989.

Best Known Songs & Scores:

Broadway Musicals: ***Ziegfeld Follies of 1919**, **Annie Get Your Gun** (1946)*
***Call Me Madam** (1950)*

Songs Featured in Movies: "Puttin' on the Ritz" (1929), **"Alexander's Ragtime Band"** (1938) **"Easter Parade"** (1948), **"Anything You Can Do"** (1950), **"There's No Business Like Show Business"** (1954), **"White Christmas"** (1954)

Songs: "God Bless America", "Steppin' Out with My Baby", "Blue Skies" "Always", "Cheek to Cheek", "What'll I Do?"

Review: Lesson 11

1. Fill in the correct answer(s) to the following questions about Frederick Loewe & Irving Berlin.

Frederick Loewe

a. Frederick Loewe was born in which country? ________________________

b. He represents the __________________________period of music.

c. What is the name of the musical he wrote in 1956 that starred Julie Andews in the part of

Eliza Doolittle? _______________________________________

d. Who was the lyricist with whom Loewe collaborated with on several musicals, including *Gigi*?

____

e. Name the musical that also starred Julie Andrews, which included the characters King

Arthur, Lancelot and Queen Guinevere. ______________________________.

Irving Berlin

a. Irving Berlin was born in which country? __________________________

b. He represents the ________________________period of music.

c. What is the name of his first hit song? ___________________________________

d. His song "A Pretty Girl is Like a Melody" was written for what musical revue in 1919?

____

e. What is the name of his patriotic song that premiered in 1938 and is still popular today?

____

Level 2 Review Test

Answer the questions about the following musical example. (15 points)

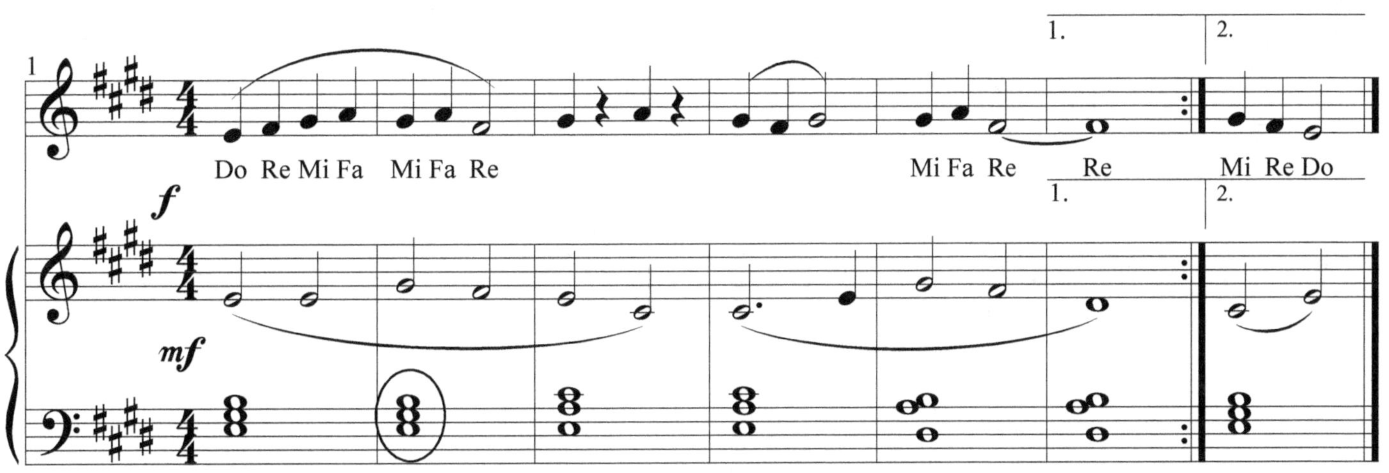

1. Which 2 measures have a tie in the vocal line? ________ & ________

2. How many slurs are in the piano accompaniment? ________

3. How should the vocal part be sung? (circle one)
   a. Loud
   b. Soft

4. Which measure contains a repeat sign? ________

5. What Major key is this song in? ________

6. What measure contains a dotted half note in the piano accompaniment? ________

7. How many beats are in each measure of this song? ________

8. Name the circled chord in measure 2. (circle one)
   B Major
   E Major

9. Name the missing solfege for measures 3 & 4 in the vocal line?

   ______ ______ ______ ______ ______

10. How many measures are sung in this song (total, including the 1st/2nd endings & repeat)? (circle one)
    12
    7

11. Write the letter names of the notes below. (20 points)

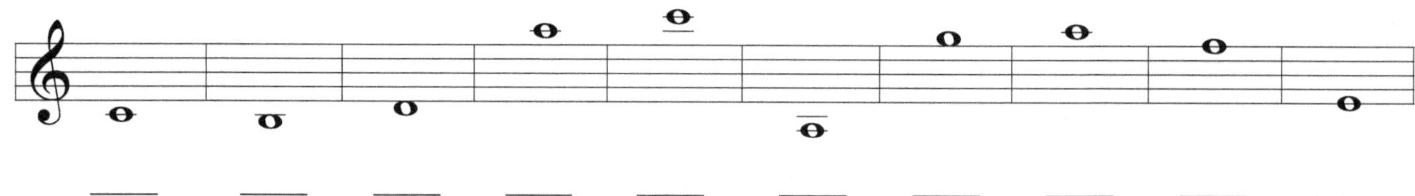

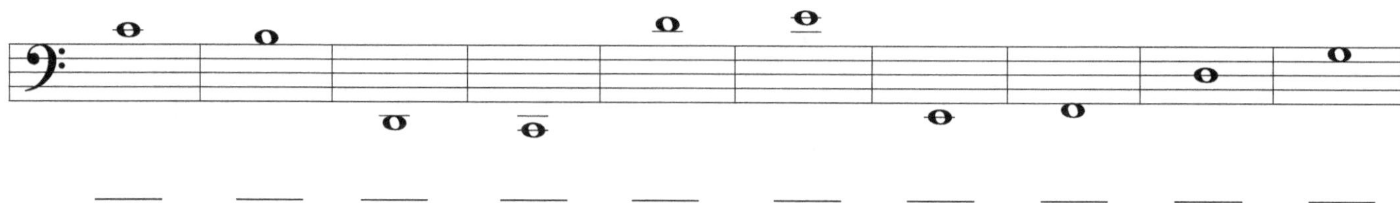

12. Name the following notes and their values *(for example: Quarter note, 1 beat)*. (12 points)

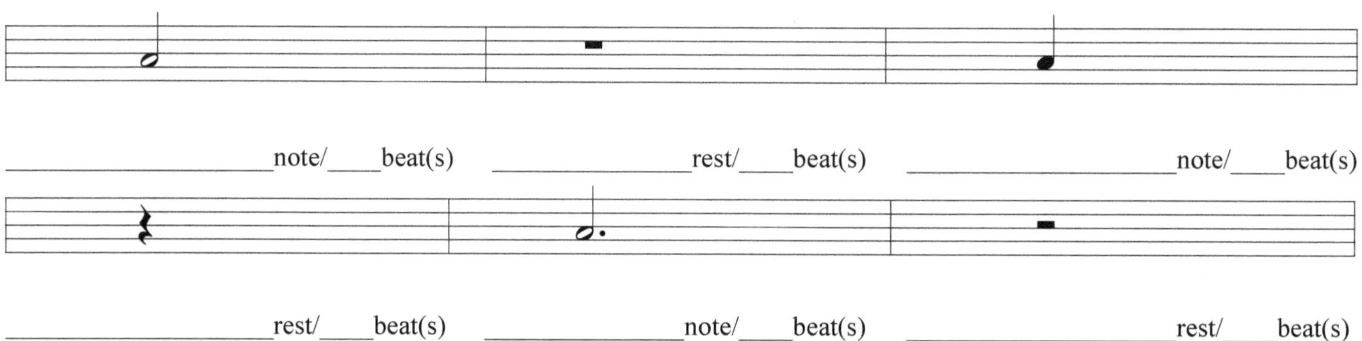

13. Name the key signature <u>and</u> interval (4th/5th) for each example. (8 points)

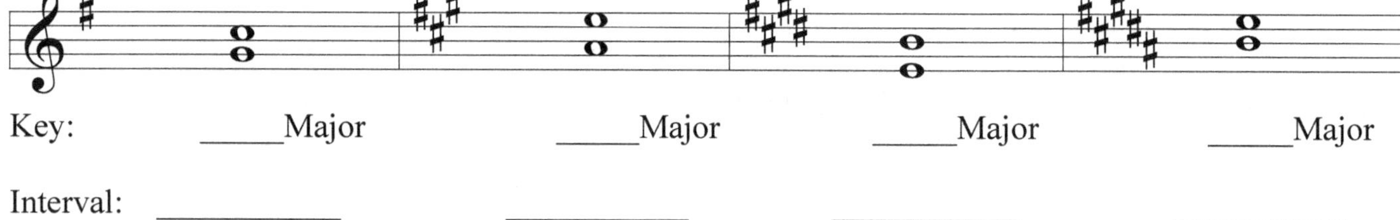

14. Each of these chords should have a Do (1), Mi (3), & Sol (5).
Fill in the missing note for each chord in both clefs to create a root position triad. (8 points)

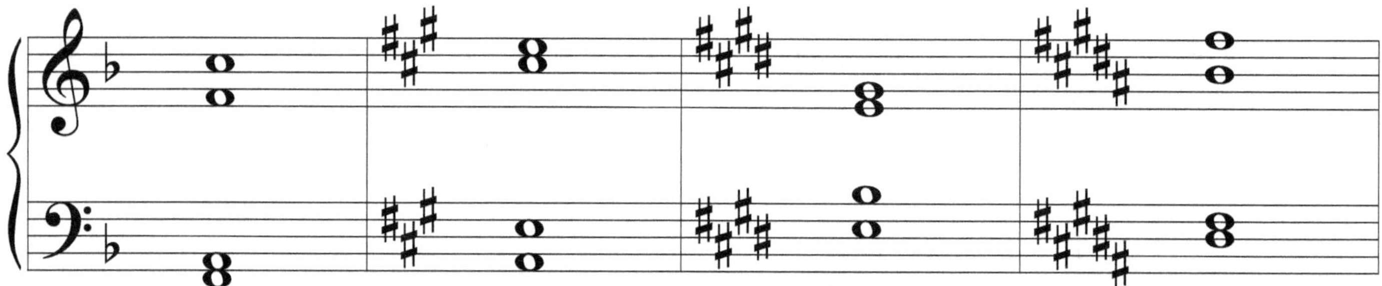

15. Write the beats under the examples. Pay attention to the time signatures!
(12 points- 1 point per correct measure)

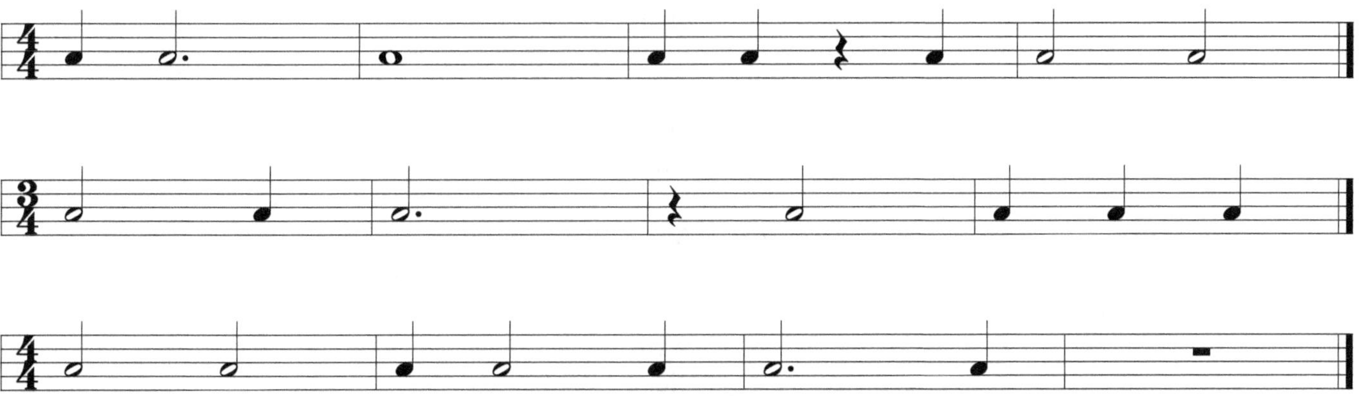

16. Write the note names and solfege directly under each note in the following examples. Don't forget to add ♯/♭ if needed. (12 points-1 point per correct measure: both solfege and notes must be correct)

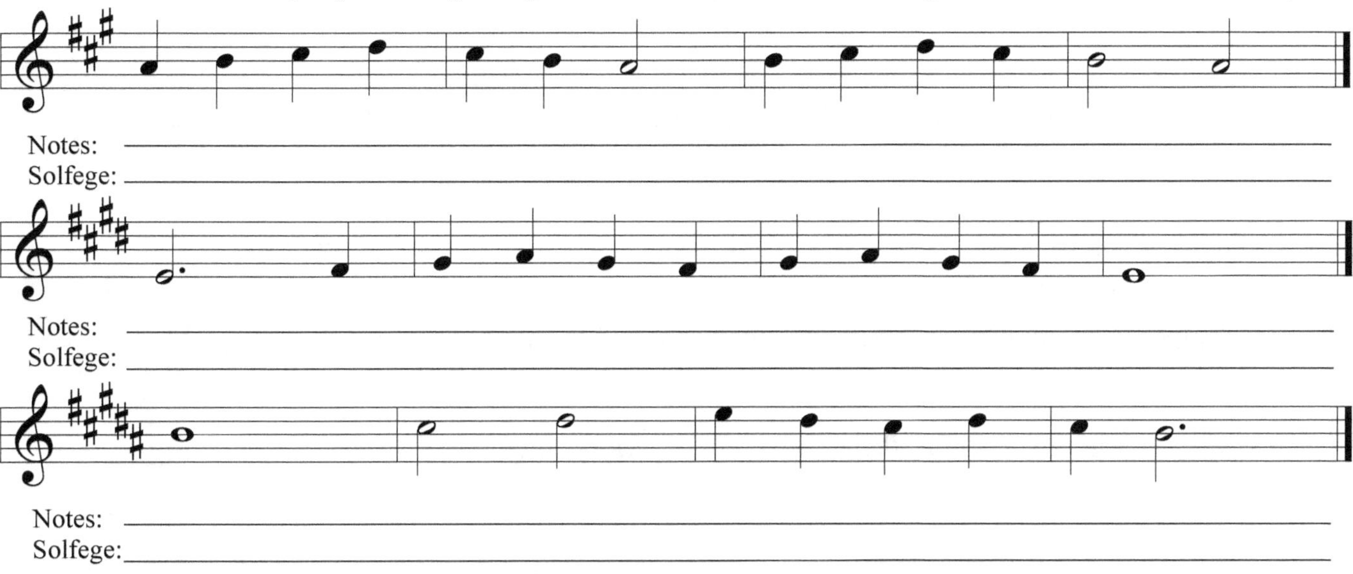

17. Fill in the correct answer using the musical terms in this level. (5 points)

a. The ____________________period of music occured between the years 1425 -1600.

b. Pianissimo means _______________________________.

c. To crescendo means to get gradually ________________.

d. Short lines added above or below the staff for additional notes are called ____________lines.

e. A ______ increases a note by half of it's value.

18. Check the English word that contains the same sound as the given IPA symbol. (5 points)

ɪ	___Fish ___White
e	___Bet ___Play
ə	___About ___Eat
i	___Wish ___Sleep
ɑ	___Pot ___Late

19. For the following questions, write "Frederick Loewe" or "Irving Berlin" as your answer. (5 points)

a. This composer died when he was 101 years old. ______________________________

b. This composer wrote over 1,500 songs before he was 30 years old.___________________________

c. This composer wrote *Camelot, Brigadoon* and *My Fair Lady.*______________________________

d. This composer was born in Russia.__________________________

e. This composer won 9 Academy awards for one of his musicals.____________________________

Final Score:__________/102

answer key begins on the next page

Level 2 Review Test: Answers

Answer the questions about the following musical example. (15 points)

1. Which 2 measures have a tie in the vocal line? 5 & 6

2. How many slurs are in the piano accompaniment? 3

3. How should the vocal part be sung? (circle one) a. Loud (circled)

4. Which measure contains a repeat sign? 6

5. What Major key is this song in? E

6. What measure contains a dotted half note? 4

7. How many beats are in each measure of this song? 4

8. Name the circled chord in measure 2. (circle one) B Major / E Major (circled)

9. Name the missing solfege for measures 3 & 4 in the vocal line?

Mi Fa Mi Re Mi

10. How many measures are sung in this song (total, including the 1st/2nd endings & repeat)? (circle one) 12 (circled) / 7

11. Write the letter names of the notes below. (20 points)

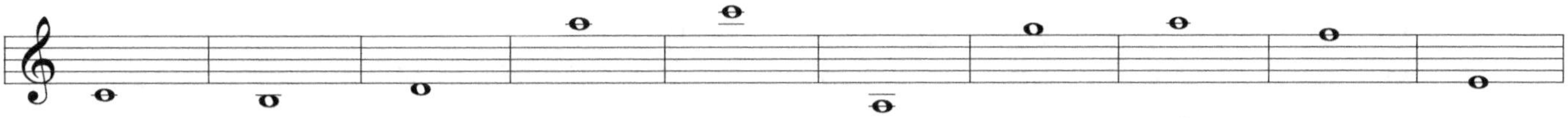

Treble clef: C B D A C A G A F E

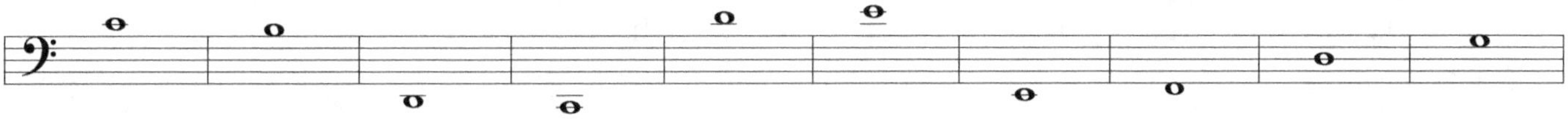

Bass clef: C B D C D E E F D G

12. Name the following notes and their values *(for example: Quarter note, 1 beat)*. (12 points)

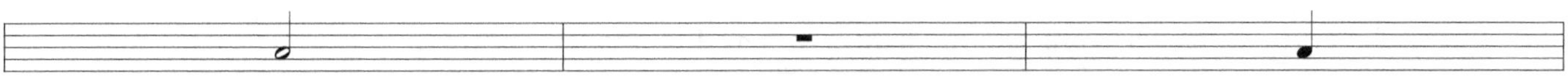

Half note/2 beats

Whole rest/4 beats

Quarter note/1 beat

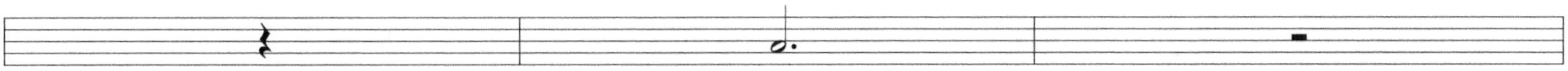

Quarter rest/1beat

Dotted half note/3 beats

Half rest/2 beats

13. Name the key signature <u>and</u> interval (4th/5th) for each example. (8 points)

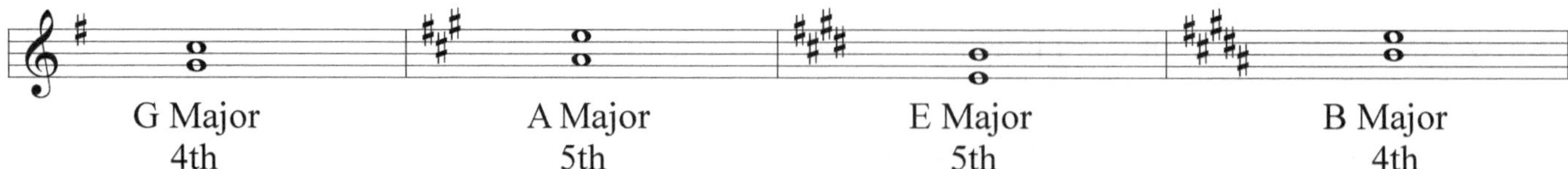

14. Each of these chords should have a Do (1), Mi (3), & Sol (5).
Fill in the missing note for each chord in both clefs to create a root position triad. (8 points)

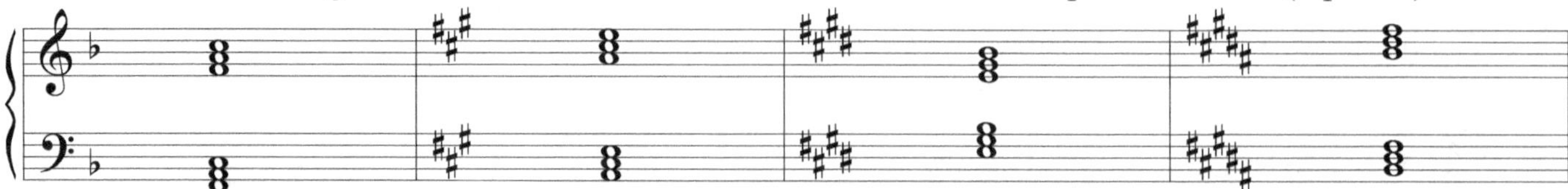

15. Write the beats under the examples. Pay attention to the time signatures!
(12 points- 1 point per correct measure)

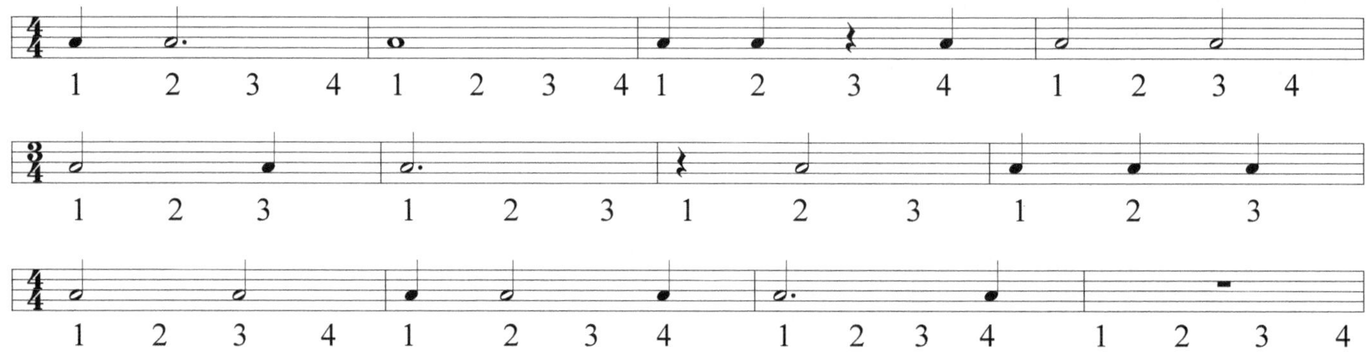

16. Write the note names and solfege under each note in the following examples. Don't forget to add ♯/♭ if needed. (12 points-1 point per correct measure: both solfege and notes must be correct)

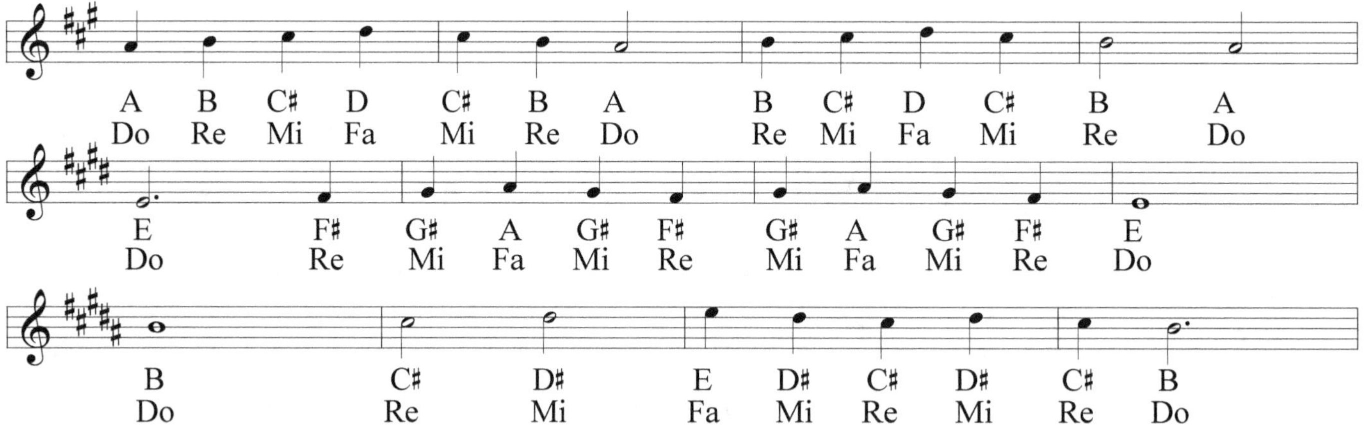

17. Fill in the correct answer using the musical terms in this level. (5 points)

a. Renaissance
b. very soft
c. louder
d. ledger
e. dot

18. Check the English word that contains the same sound as the given IPA symbol. (5 points)

ɪ - Fish

e - Play

ə - About

i - Sleep

ɑ - Pot

19. For the following questions, write "Frederick Loewe" or "Irving Berlin" as your answer. (5 points)

a. This composer died when he was 101 years old. Irving Berlin

b. This composer wrote over 1,500 songs before he was 30 years old. Irving Berlin

c. This composer wrote *Camelot, Brigadoon* and *My Fair Lady.* Frederick Loewe

d. This composer was born in Russia. Irving Berlin

e. This composer won 9 Academy awards for one of his musicals. Frederick Loewe

REFERENCES

Grout, Donald. *A History of Western Music.* New York, NY: W.W. Norton & Company, Inc., 1996.

Moriarty, John. *Diction*. Boston, MA: E. C. Schirmer Music Company, 1975.

Music Teachers' Association of California. *Certificate of Merit Voice Syllabus.* San Francisco: Music Teachers' Association of California, 2011.

Piston, Walter. *Harmony, Fifth Edition.* New York, NY: W.W. Norton & Company, Inc., 1987.

Plantinga, Leon. *Romantic Music, A History of Musical Style in Nineteenth-Century Europe.* New York, NY: W.W. Norton & Company, Inc., 1984.

Randel, Don Michael. *The Harvard Biographical Dictionary of Music.* Cambridge, Massachusetts: The Belknap Press of Harvard University Press, 1996.

Randel, Don Michael. *Harvard Concise Dictionary of Music.* Cambridge, Massachusetts: The Belknap Press of Harvard University Press, 1978.

Rushton, Julian. *Classical Music, A Concise History from Gluck to Beethoven.* London, England: Thames and Hudson Ltd., 1986.

The New Grove Dictionary of Music and Musicians. http://www.oxfordmusiconline.com., 2011

www.ingramcontent.com/pod-product-compliance
Lightning Source LLC
LaVergne TN
LVHW061257100826
845148LV00008B/1152

* 9 7 8 1 5 2 4 9 1 4 3 7 0 *